Dream Big

Dream Big

An Irishwoman's Space Odyssey

NIAMH SHAW

MERCIER PRESS

MERCIER PRESS

Cork

www.mercierpress.ie

© Niamh Shaw, 2020

ISBN: 978 1 78117 715 0

A CIP record for this title is available from the British Library.

Printed and bound in the EU.

Here's to the *Earthrise* picture and to those involved in getting us to the Moon in 1969 – for inspiring so many of us to see the world differently.

There are no borders or boundaries on our planet except those that we create in our minds or through human behaviours. All the ideas and concepts that divide us when we are on the surface begin to fade from orbit and the Moon. The result is a shift in world view, and in our identity.

– Carl Sagan

Contents

Prologue

Where are you right now? I imagine you are probably in a room in your house, or on a train or bus, or a plane, or even a boat. Maybe you're outside in your garden, or on a park bench in the city. Right now, I'm sitting on my couch, which I have moved to face my back yard (it helps me to write if I can see a bit of nature). We're both in different places, but wherever we are, we are occupying a piece of space on our planet.

What city or town are you in? I'm in Dublin. Let's zoom out a bit more. What country are you in right now? While I can hope that this book will be read globally, I'm going to conservatively estimate that we're both in Ireland right now (if not, please email me; I'll be thrilled to hear from an overseas reader). Ireland is 84,421 square kilometres and occupies 0.7 per cent of Europe, which is 10.8 million square kilometres in size. Yet Europe occupies just two per cent of Earth's surface, the total area of which is 510.1 million square kilometres. And we occupy such a teeny tiny part of that. And we are all aware of that. As we sit, stand or lie, wherever we are, we are a tiny part of this planet.

If it's daytime while you're reading this, take a look up (or out) at the sky. It's pretty bright, isn't it? The light is coming from the Sun, which I'm sure you already know. The Sun is roughly 149 million kilometres away from you right now. In fact, the light that you can see is light that left our sun eight minutes ago. Which means that if the Sun decided to down tools and shut off for the day, our sky wouldn't darken for eight minutes.

Let's zoom out further. The Sun is one of millions of stars in our local interstellar neighbourhood, the nearest of which, Alpha Centauri, is 4.3 light years away (a light year is 9.46 trillion kilometres). And all of this is part of one galaxy, the Milky Way, which is 100,000 light years in diameter. Meanwhile, the Milky Way is one galaxy of hundreds of other galaxies grouped together in a cluster called the Virgo Cluster. These clusters are grouped into superclusters. There are fifty-five superclusters within the observable universe, the edge of which is 46.6 billion light years away from us.

Right now.

And that's where we are. As you sit, stand or lie there, reading this book.

And that's just what we know today. There is so much more to know and to explore.

The urge to explore starts from when we take our first steps. For some, that exploration never ends. After all, the universe is a big place and we've always been trying to define our place in it. From the Egyptians or the Aztecs worshipping the Sun, to the Chinese naming the stars, or the Babylonians inventing astrology, we have always been connecting our lives to the cosmos. The stars have been our gods; they have guided us. They have inspired our calendars and almanacs, and all the while we believed ourselves secure, at the centre of an orderly universe.

Then, in 1608, with the invention of the telescope, we realised it was our planet orbiting the Sun, not vice versa. And in 1610 Galileo discovered that our star was part of a much bigger system of stars, a galaxy. Not until the 1920s did we realise that there were other galaxies out there, hundreds of them. And only twenty years ago did we discover that our solar system, our planetary system, wasn't unique; there are, in fact, as many as forty billion planetary systems.

And that's just what we know today.

The more we look at the skies, the smaller we become. How simple a life would be without questions, if we didn't need to know. But we do need to know. Since the dawn of time, humans have been curious, have always wanted to know what lies over the hill. The urge to explore is an inherent part of who we are. If we know anything we know one thing: we NEED to know.

And I NEED to know too.

People's lives from the outside all seem so well planned, don't they? Well, I can tell you now, for me, that couldn't be further from the truth. I wish life were that simple. Because the real story of my life is quite different. I have been haunted by my dream to go to space my whole life.

Even when I was lost in life, I always knew that I was destined for something bigger. Unfortunately, I forgot what that destiny was for a very long time. But in the very back of my mind, my subconscious kept that hope and dream safe, locked away in a vault, for the day when I would be ready to share it with myself again.

Life would have been a whole lot simpler if I had been brave enough to devote all my life to this one quest. But that isn't my story. I went along a number of paths in my life only to end up back where I was when I was eight years old, deciding what I wanted to be. It's exhausting to deny yourself the right to be who you truly are.

I'm Niamh Shaw and I want to go to space. And this is my story.

Author's Note:

Brief extracts from my stage plays, *That's About the Size of It* and *To Space*, appear in italics throughout the book. In some cases, stage directions are included. Furthermore, QR codes (as above) are included throughout the text. These will provide you with links to footage and relevant information pertaining to my journey.

Part 1

On Hold

Hi, I'm Niamh.

*When I was very young, I wanted to be an astronaut
or a ballerina. I could never decide.*

*No one remembers that I wanted to be an astronaut or
a ballerina.*

*My parents say that I wanted to be a doctor or a
teacher.*

*My nana wanted me to be a hairdresser, or a nurse,
and my auntie wanted me to be a linguist.*

I told people what they wanted to hear.

Because they loved me.

And then I forgot what I wanted to be.

I waited for people to tell me.

– Excerpt from *That's About the Size of It*, 2011

Chapter 1

Submerged

It's March 2001 and I'm living in Mull's Cottage in Cork. It's a beautiful cottage on half an acre of land just beyond Bishopstown. I have my very own vegetable patch, a bird table and three outdoor sheds. It's the type of house I've always dreamed of living in. If I can ever afford to buy my own house, it will be something like Mull's Cottage. I love living here and yet I'm utterly miserable.

It's about 8 p.m., I think. I'm lying on the terracotta tiles. I know that something has to change. But that comes later. Now, I am broken and have finally allowed myself to let go, to stop trying to make everything work, to stop pretending that I'm satisfied with this life. Because I'm not.

I don't know what to do next. Lying on the floor seems like the most appealing thing to do. It's in the corridor between the living room and kitchen area and the two bedrooms and bathroom. I submitted my PhD just three months earlier, when everything seemed so promising. My first job, at University College Cork (UCC) Food Science and Technology, had been secured. No more third-level education; those years as a student finally over. There was supposed to be a reward for years of scrimping through life, the long hours, all the supervision, the months spent in isolation, researching, testing, recording, analysing, writing. The thesis. The cost of that commitment and how it had impacted on my personal life: the events I missed, the people I didn't see. All of it. Now it was supposed to get easier. But that's not what has happened.

I'm exhausted. I feel that I've had a painted-on smile all this time. And the smile has now dropped, only to be replaced with anger and fear. I'm broken-hearted. What was it all for?

I have no one. I've pushed everyone away. I hid behind the work to remain isolated, safe in the sort of solitude where no one can hurt you, or disappoint you, or reject you. It worked for such a long time. But now it all feels wrong.

My hands are loosely beside my head, and my right cheek is touching a cold tile. There's a small rug in my line of sight: the typical Persian style of reds and browns and a thin string of tassel fringing. I'm staring at it and not really thinking about much. I just feel numb. I want to lie here forever and stare at the fringing. It feels like I've discovered a secret level of existence, where I'm no longer in my life but in a sub-existence. My life is continuing about half a metre above me, but I'm hiding on the terracotta tiles. And if I lie here maybe I won't be discovered. Maybe I can let the fake Niamh cover for me, let her keep on smiling with her forced smile, keep working away at the food technology department at UCC, keep eating, keep sleeping, keep living this fake life in which she has trapped herself.

Everything seems different from the terracotta tiles. I see a spider emerge from the bathroom, pause briefly by the rug, and then continue on his journey towards the bedroom, moving along the edge of the corridor, staying close to the skirting board, pausing occasionally and then moving again. He's a small spider: short legs, with not much hair. Not particularly scary. On the scale of spiders, he's pretty forgettable. I wonder if he is strutting right now, or scurrying? To me, he seems confident, pretty sure of what he's about. How simple life must be, I imagine, when you are a spider. What's he thinking about? Does he have a big plan for his life, for where he is going? Does he want to settle down, make baby spiders? Has he made a permanent home somewhere for himself? If so, does it have all the modern conveniences befitting a spider at his stage of development? Or is he a free spirit spider, without a care in the world, creating a life for himself off the 'spider grid'? He seems to have it all figured out. I want to follow his example for a bit. Not plan. Not think. Just stay still.

Switch off.

Check out.

Let go.

Fall. Fall. Fall.

Give in.

Just give in.

I want to stay here, half a metre below the real world. How delicious that would be.

***

I wake up. My body is tense from the cold of the terracotta tiles. I need to get up, but I want to remain in the haze that

I've been in; it's comforting. You don't need to think in the haze, or focus on anything.

I'm stiff when I stand. Deciding what to do or where to go next is difficult, because a part of me is still trying not to think.

I stare at the tassels again. I don't really want to move, but I need to get warm.

I run a bath in darkness. I light a candle and get in. And lie there. In the haze once again. The coldness creeps towards me: at first it's in the air, then the line between the water and the air, and then in the water itself.

There's a man in my life. I think. But he promises me nothing except his company. I decide to drive over to his place. He's studying in his apartment a few miles away. I've been leaning on him too much recently to fill the void. After I arrive, he continues to study and I look at his goldfish. He knows that something is up, and knows to just leave me to myself. One of the goldfish is eleven years old, or so he says. The eleven-year-old goldfish certainly looks old; he's big enough. This goldfish does a nice thing where he picks up one of the little stones at the bottom of the tank, sucks on it and releases it, before picking up another one to suck. There must be algae on the stones. Both fish are oblivious to me watching them.

When he's done studying, the man suggests that we go for a drink. And once out, socialising, I rise the half metre to my life again, engaging in chat, distracting myself for a while. It's soon closing time, however, and I have to go back home. I don't want to be alone, but I don't tell him that.

I drive the six kilometres back to my cottage. Close the door. Return to the terracotta tiles for a while, but eventually get into bed.

All I know is that something needs to change. Otherwise I'm going to drown in this haze.

The more we study the universe,
the more that is revealed and the more complex it gets.

In 1990, the American Space Agency, NASA, and ESA
(the European Space Agency)
launched a telescope called the Hubble telescope,
which continues to orbit Earth to this day.
Located about 300km above us, this was a telescope that
was launched into space.
And a telescope in space far surpasses ground-based tele-
scopes because our atmosphere distorts and blocks the light
that reaches our planet.

The Hubble telescope sent back images of our universe that
we had never seen before, with unprecedented clarity and
accuracy.
Images of
gas clouds,
nebulae,
supernovas.
This telescope, this perspective, has revolutionised our
understanding of the universe.

Then, in 2003, NASA pointed the Hubble telescope
towards a dark point in the sky just south-west of the

*constellation Orion and took a really long photograph, a
three-month-long exposure, that allowed them to see into
the darkness
and slowly reveal the light.*

*Much like the way our eyes adjust when we enter a dark
room,
the longer we wait
the more light we see.*

*The Hubble used this long exposure to illuminate that
dark patch of sky
and revealed
10,000 galaxies
in that tiny piece of darkness.
10,000 galaxies that could each be home to 300 billion
stars.*

*In the three months that it took to take that really long
photograph,
our knowledge of the universe expanded by
10,000 galaxies,
three trillion stars.*

*And these galaxies, we know,
are approximately 13.1 billion years old.
Which means that the light that the Hubble telescope was
receiving
was 13.1 billion years old.*

*What is so magnificent about this
is that if you or I were to stand on the top of a hill
and identify the constellation Orion*

and point to the south-west corner,
to a dark patch of sky about 1mm by 1mm in size at the
tip of our finger,
we now know that
we're pointing at the past,
we're pointing at the first stars ever created,
we're pointing at the edge of the universe,
the last remaining light from the Big Bang travelling
towards us.
We're pointing at the past,
we're looking at the past.
Our past.

– Excerpt from *To Space, 2014*

Chapter 2

The Scholar

I'm not sure how accurate memories of our childhoods can be. Seemingly, every time we recall a memory, it changes. So I'll try to give you the highlights as accurately as I can. I don't believe that I had some sort of destiny. All I've ever done is plod along, and definitely for the earlier part of my life I didn't really have a plan. All I knew was that I liked facts, I loved thinking, I liked to talk, I loved being in love and I thought that space was fascinating. So with all that in mind, here's how I remember things.

My upbringing was pretty decent. I grew up in a house where education was the priority and knowledge had currency. I was lucky, I know that. It was a strict house, but we were inspired to be curious in every way possible. I'm the third child in the family: there's Deirdre, who's the eldest, then John, me and Tom. Regardless of our gender, we were all encouraged to do well in school and to prepare ourselves for a college education. Dad showed me how to wire a plug, connect up the television to the stereo system, plant potatoes and keep tomatoes. Mam was also a strong presence in the house and was just as capable as Dad of getting stuff done. We worked together on so many DIY projects around the house. We weren't the kind of family who had a SodaStream,

Swingball or summer holidays abroad, as much as we pleaded. We were a family of *Encyclopaedia Britannica*, history books, gadgets, screwdrivers, spare batteries, fuses and caravan breaks to Banna Strand in Co. Kerry with our aunts and uncles and cousins. We were shown *Life on Earth* with David Attenborough, and *Cosmos* with Carl Sagan, as well as a ton of whatever science fiction we could access. This was my world (with a few Sindy dolls and a bit of *Charlie's Angels* thrown in for good measure). It was a pretty delicious world for a family of learners.

Deirdre, John and I are all gingers and in the 1980s that wasn't cool. I'm not sure if it is even now! We got slagged a lot as kids for being ginger. 'Your hair's on fire.' 'Hey tomato head.' I heard them all, especially from boys hanging out together. Idiots. They were so lame. It never bothered me when I was alone, but when we were together, the other kids were like a pack of wolves, snarling out insults. Once we hit puberty we realised that we were exponentially less cool when seen together, so we didn't hang out together in public for years!

One Christmas we got a Sinclair ZX Spectrum for the whole family. This was one of the early forms of home computer, used for the first generation of gaming, essentially. But you had to write the programs yourself, or at least transcribe them from magazines such as *PC World*, because there was no memory on the computer to store the games. With a capacity of a mere 16 kilobytes, you connected this keyboard (the computer) to your TV, typed in the code, connected the keyboard to a tape recorder, and then hit RUN on the computer. I'm still not sure how that made the games run, but it did! They were invariably pretty pedestrian. Inevitably, the first time you hit RUN you would receive a program error, because there was a typo on one of the lines of code, or some other error code. I was always determined to figure out where that error was. Even if it took me hours, I would stick at it until I found the error. Dad says that's when he knew that I was an engineer. I would get more of a thrill from fixing the error than from the game itself. For me, that's when I realised I had a logical mind. And that I really enjoyed using it.

Mam is from a family of trad musicians and performers, so from a very young age we were used to people singing together, sharing stories and reciting poetry. Performance came easy to me at that age. I always enjoyed the process of preparing something and then sharing it. I wrote Christmas shows every year with Deirdre; a series of sketches about preparing for Christmas, with scene changes and props. They always ended with a song, which was usually one of Deirdre's favourite carols. (Allowing her to sing was the only way that I could rope her in to performing the sketches with me.)

Having said that, I could also be painfully shy, particularly outside my family circle. I found it difficult to make new friends, and I often preferred my own company rather than taking the risk of trusting someone new. It took me a long time to let people in, even at that age. As a result, I mostly hung out with my family; it seemed easier that way.

John in particular was a big inspiration to me. He's three years older than me. As a boy, he had oodles of energy, and was always reading, thinking and sharing his ideas with us all. His love of space spilled over onto me, I guess. Whenever Dad got a free poster from his *National Geographic* subscription, he'd give it to us. Some were of the 'Kings & Queens of England' or 'Evolution of our Species', but I particularly loved the solar system posters. John would tell me about the Milky Way, our solar system, black holes, red dwarfs, collapsing stars, Alpha Centauri and the possibility of alien life. I liked it when he spent time with me, as I usually played on my own. He even used some of his confirmation money to take me and Tom to see *Star Wars* for the first time.

***

Cinema.
Carlow.
Small town. Midlands.
1977.
Smell of stale smoke. Popcorn.
Burgundy seats.
Burgundy carpet.
Burgundy walls.
Like I said.
Carlow. 1977.

Empty.

There's a boy. Four.
In front of the screen.

Fair.

Straight hair.
Playing Dinky cars.
Saliva. Ugh!

There's another boy. Eleven.
Red hair.
Frizzy.
Big freckles. Almost joining up.
Nerdy. Intelligent.
He reads encyclopaedias.

For fun.

Excited. Jumping up and down on the seats. Ridiculously excited.

And a girl in between.
Eight.
Red hair. Short.
Cut by her mother.
Freckles. Smaller freckles than brother.
Makes her feel superior.

I like this girl.
She's good at Maths.
Not so good at Nature.
She likes her Mickey Mouse watch.
She's afraid of the dark.
She mows lawns.
She buries cats.
She's a bad knitter.

Movie begins.

Eyes widen, heart beats faster.
This is great – this is the best thing she has ever seen!
She likes Princess Leia.
She wants her hair.
She likes Han Solo.

He's so dreamy.
Chewbacca, C3PO, yeah whatever.
But she'd love her own R2D2.

She thinks Luke Skywalker is a complete doofus, ugh.
Why is he the star of this movie?

Ah, the Millennium Falcon.
She appreciates this.
Such great design.
The propulsion systems.
Its ability to travel at light speed
through the galaxies.
A superb piece of engineering.

It reminds her of the poster in her brother's room
of the Milky Way
and Alpha Centauri
and our solar system.
She wants to be a part of this.

'Hey, John, I want to be an astronaut!'
I'm eight years old and
I want to be an astronaut.

– Excerpt from *To Space*, 2014

***

The *Earthrise* picture fascinated me at that age (it still does). Taken on Christmas Eve 1968 by Apollo 8 astronaut William (Bill) Anders, it was the very first time that our planet was captured in its entirety. Seeing that photograph of Earth, in half-light and from the perspective of the Moon, was stunning. I'm not surprised that this image changed people's perception of our existence and kick-started environmental movements to protect our delicate planet. I first saw it in the *Children's Encyclopaedia,* probably around the age of eight or so. This is where the dream began. Whenever I imagine my mission to space, that's the view I'm aiming for – seeing Earth in its entirety.

I kept diaries a lot during this period, and I'm so glad that I still have them. I'm transported back to being that nine-year-old, or twelve-year-old, or fifteen-year-old, or twenty-four-year-old. They have been a useful resource for me when making my theatre shows (and in writing this book).

We moved house a lot from 1976 to 1981 as Dad was moving up the ranks of the various engineering firms where he worked, which meant that I went to four different primary schools in five years. Walking into a classroom as the new girl can be tough. While I am inherently shy, I learned fast how to get to know new people. I became the comedian and was well liked by my classmates, by and large. It was a pretty successful method of settling into a new class – except on our last move to Dundalk.

This final move from Lucan to Dundalk took place in my sixth-class year. In order for me to attend St Louis Secondary

School the following September, I first had to attend their primary, Scoil Eoin Baiste, for five months from January 1981. It was a very long five months. I had been a fairly confident child and pretty content with who I was prior to my arrival, but I got a big dollop of reality when I was in Scoil Eoin Baiste.

Looking back on it now, it's fair to say that I was bullied by more than half of that class. My self-esteem was obliterated within those five short months. And I wouldn't necessarily blame the girls; it turned out that they hated me before I even got there. This was a school that was barely surviving, stretched to capacity, fulfilling its duty to provide a basic primary education for people within its catchment area. It was just an ordinary school, not especially aspiring for academic excellence, and yet the principal kept bragging that a girl from 'Dublin' would soon be joining their class – so really I was a dead woman walking before I even set foot in the school.

I remember the first time someone tried to push me around. I went home that evening and prepared a whole speech that I would give to her the next day, explaining how it wasn't acceptable for her to treat me that way. I didn't get to have that chat with her, though, as I decided to let it pass. I needed to settle in first, not ruffle any feathers. But within a matter of weeks, things got a whole lot worse – people would squash oranges in my face, trip me up, push me, laugh at me, mock my accent, my red hair, my appearance and generally make me the butt of everything that happened in our class. And I let them. I would laugh along, pretending that I enjoyed the mocking.

But inwardly I was crushed. No one really wanted to hang out with me, or sit beside me, or be connected with me in any way. I still managed to have one or two quasi-friends in that class, but I wasn't in control of the rules of the friendship. Not that I overly cared; I was happy to have any company.

Our teacher had little or no control over the class. She would scream at us, and sometimes cry with frustration when she couldn't settle us down. The girls would just laugh at her. She started to single me out and punish me for the group behaviour, probably because I was one of the few students whom she could still control. I felt completely alone in that room and knew that I had to rely on myself to survive. Kill or be killed. One day I snapped and gave her a mouthful of attitude back, which I remember went down well with the bullies.

Overall, it was a miserable few months and the part that I'm most ashamed of when I look back on it was that I often helped these bullies during exams. They would whisper across to me, asking for answers to questions, which I gladly gave. I hoped that they would be nicer to me if I helped them. When they weren't directly attacking me, I would keep trying to be their friend.

Before Scoil Eoin Baiste, I had never doubted who I was. In a way, it had been a gift. I'm thankful that this was the only school that I attended where I experienced bullying. While all the girls from that class also went on to St Louis', our paths never really crossed again. But neither did I ever really regain my self-esteem to the same degree.

I'm not sure if I ever dealt with it all. I told my mother about it at the time, but what could she do? She largely ignored the situation; she was too busy taking care of us all. It was my responsibility to manage myself.

I hated going to school for the first time in my life. But, thankfully, secondary school was to be a lot better.

Dundalk.
1982.
Alarm – 8 a.m.
Cold bedroom. Can see your breath.
Frost on the windows.

White vest and shirt. And green.
Green skirt.
Green tie.
Green blazer.
Green socks – get two days out of them.
Black Clarks shoes.

Lunch.
Sardines on white bread
or
corned beef on white bread
or
cheese and cucumber on white bread.
Wrapped in O'Brien's bread paper.

School.
Bell.
Walk on left of stairs! Sssh!

Prayers.
Science lab.
Cold.
Brown benches.
Formaldehyde smell.
Like it.
Like the hardback copies.
Graph paper on one side, lined on the other.
Titrations. Stoichiometry.
Ms Greer: tough, fair, encouraging.
Fascinating.

Lunch.
Cloakroom.
Classes.

3.50 p.m.

Home.
Mam's watching Countdown.
Dinner in oven.
Tinfoil. Plate too hot. Burns my hand. Ouch!
Dried potato scoops and crinkley peas.
Pork Chop Monday
Mince Tuesday
Stew Wednesday
Gammon Steak Thursday.
Brown sauce.
Lots of brown sauce.
Fridays we have egg and chips.
Yum!

Homework.
Meticulous.
Always completed.
The Byzantine era,
the First World War,
Tutankhamun.
John's right
or Dad's right.
Encyclopaedia to check.
Dad was once always right.

Tea.
TV.
Charlie's Angels.
Six Million Dollar Man.
Star Trek.
Cosmos *with Carl Sagan.*
Life on Earth *with David Attenborough.*
And ugh, news!

Prayers.
Always in the middle of our favourite show.

Bedroom window.
Lace curtains.
Watching.
Waiting.
For school.

School. Home. Repeat.
School. Home. Repeat.

Until one day. Mr Barr.
Niamh, can I have a word?
A play?
A ghost play?
Are you sure, sir?

Me and Linda McQuaid taking lead, taking charge –
finding props, writing scripts. Until lunchtime. School
Hall. 31 May 1982. 10p admission please!
Excited, nervous. Giggling with the gang off stage.
We begin.
I stand on stage, nerves disappear. I say the lines and this
feels right!
I like people looking at me! Fifty-seven in the audience.
All looking at me, listening to me.
Laughter. Applause.
We did it. I love it. This feels right. This is what I want to
do.

Home.
Mam. Dad. The play …
– Eat your dinner!
Mam. Dad. I want …
– Have you done your homework?
But the play. I want …
– Homework Niamh! Tests Niamh! Study Niamh!

Bed.
Waiting.

To Sleep. To Dream.

– Excerpt from *To Space*, 2014

Chapter 3

Growing Up

In general, I loved being a pupil at St Louis'. I loved the subjects and the way every class was forty minutes long, as well as the variety of teachers we had for different subjects. It was so glamorous to me, what with all the books I needed to get (to then cover with scrap bits of wallpaper), the copybooks, the stationery, the homework notebooks. I loved it all.

I particularly loved to study science, as it immediately made sense to me. I loved how it explained the world by breaking it up into digestible packets of information. And I was lucky to have three teachers whose passion for their subjects spilled over and into my lap: Mrs Greer for chemistry, Mr Kelly for physics and Sr Louis Marie for English and drama.

My teenage years were all about living through my friends – you can see it in my diaries. I wasn't particularly anarchic or anything, in fact I was still pretty nerdy, but I lived for all our teenage dramas. It was the first time that I actually wanted friends, or needed them. Success to me was having a boyfriend and feeling attractive. Lots of my friends had all that. Rather than share my love of funk over new romantic, sci-fi over *Dallas*, Kenny Everett over *The Young Ones* – I learned to suppress it all, to fit in and be just like the girls I wanted to be. It worked most of the time, but as I got older,

I started to think more and more about the purpose of my existence. There had to be more to life than this, surely? Staying busy was helpful, and that was what I did most of the time: studying, taking on extra activities like the Young Scientist Exhibition, helping out around the school. But most of the time, while I seemed happy on the outside, deep down I was pretty miserable.

As I approached the Leaving Cert, there didn't seem to be anything to look forward to. I started to stop caring about school. Something was shifting in me. Mam was worried. She told me that she loved me (which was very unusual for the 1980s). She even offered to mix up her home cooking to add more spontaneity to our weekly menu, which had remained the same for ten years. I'm not sure what it was, what caused this slump – maybe it was the teenage state of mind, of feeling misunderstood – but that apathy didn't feel good. I had been used to a regular routine of working hard and performing well in exams. That had always brought me satisfaction. When that no longer worked, it was scary for me. But then I got a boyfriend. Success at last! Everything got better after that, or so it seemed.

***

Choosing a course to pursue in college was tough for me. I studied the information as best I could but never found a course that covered all the subjects I enjoyed. A part of me wanted to do a science or engineering degree, but I also really wanted to do the communications course at Dublin City

University (DCU). I even looked at the aeronautical degree programme at the University of Limerick, the only course that was remotely related to space, but it looked far too tough for me. As much as I enjoy maths, I don't feel that I have a natural aptitude for it. I didn't think that I would succeed at aeronautical engineering – though, in hindsight, maybe I was simply terrified of failing. It would have also meant moving to Limerick. All my friends would be in Dublin, including my boyfriend. That was the deal breaker. In the end, I got enough points for both communications at DCU (then NIHE Glasnevin) and the aeronautical engineering course in Limerick. But I chose Dublin and I chose engineering at UCD.

Dundalk was the epicentre of my world at that time. Heading to the shopping centre every Saturday was the highlight of the week, or meeting outside the courthouse after school. That's where anybody who was anybody would be. And I was there, among them. As a result, the first few months after starting college in Dublin were tough; I found it difficult to adjust. I mostly kept myself to myself. There were way too many people to get to know, anyway, with 250 fellow first-year engineers, though just twenty-five of us made up the female portion. The Dublin people hung out together, while the country people seemed to already have friends. I therefore relied a lot on my friends from home. Especially my boyfriend. But I did enjoy living in Dublin. I just hadn't found my people yet. Or I was too shy to try.

My boyfriend cheated on me in the first few weeks into

our second term of college. I didn't really know how to deal with it. We talked a lot about it, but after a week or so he felt that I should be over it already. After that, I slowly began to retreat from him. As I got to know my engineering class more, I stepped away from him, from Dundalk, from the shopping centre and the square. My perception of Dundalk shifted; it was no longer the centre of my world. I realised that I had more in common with my fellow engineers, who loved sci-fi too, and maths, and facts. I didn't have to try as hard to fit in. A new world view had begun.

I worked every summer, the plan being to save up money for the following academic year, but I never really saved much. The summer after second year I went to London with some pals and when I returned that autumn for third year my perception had changed again. Zooming out further. Seeing things differently from that wider perspective.

I was a pretty average student of engineering. While I enjoyed the subjects, a lot of the time it didn't hold my full attention. My desire to be more creative had never left me. I nearly dropped out of the course in third year to study acting, but in the end I didn't dare leave, concerned always about the consequences of making the wrong decision, what people would say, going off-course. But I also stayed because I really liked hanging out with my engineer friends: their minds were similar to mine; we had lots of shared interests and perspectives.

I felt that same inner conflict during my Masters degree in engineering, which I did after spending a year travelling across Australia. I got very involved in the amateur drama scene in Dublin, participating in the one-act and three-act drama league festivals. But I never really made a genuine effort to pursue acting full-time. I did a lot of talking about it, of course, but never really committed. I stuck with what I knew; I was good at studying and delivering content – even if it was never my passion. Occasionally, however, I would have moments of clarity, moments when I knew, deep down, that I wanted more.

**

Diary Entry, 4 February 1993

I'm twenty-four tomorrow. The thought of it has sent panic through my brain all week. I mean, no matter what age you are, twenty-four sounds old and you're supposed to have everything worked out. What's so terrible in believing anything is possible?

But it isn't, is it? 'Cos the older you get, the further you are down this one-way street called a career and to be a success you've to stay on the same street. But here I am at twenty-four (almost) and I'm still at some crossroads and I still don't know which turn to make. There are so many options; I don't want to restrict myself. I want to do so much, but time limits my options as I get older. For example, if I wanted to be a successful actress, by the time I'd know everything, I'd be too old to use my full youthful potential.

Here's a list of what I want to do in the next month if I could:

Jump off a plane freefalling

Sit on a mountain for three months

Be really famous

Be an astronaut

Fall in love

When you're young time is always with you, everything you learn is added time, saved up so that you can do it twice as fast, but somewhere along the way you cross this line where doing new things becomes negative time and you're under pressure by everyone to stop learning and make use of what you already know.

***

Having said that, I really enjoyed certain aspects of doing my PhD after I completed my Masters. There was a regularity to life that was reassuring. You're in a safe bubble, so to speak; you have this big project that you know is going to take at least three years to complete. It was nice not having to think about my future for a while. There was a clear path ahead.

I moved across to science in my PhD. My previous degrees in engineering were in biological systems (known as biosystems), and my new department focused on food science topics, so the fields were at least related. It was funded for three years, though it took me four to complete.

I treated it like a full-time job, putting in at least forty to fifty hours a week. I really liked my topic. I was exploring biodegradable packaging methods using one of the two proteins in milk – whey – to form them. After an extensive review of the literature, and the assistance of a brilliant post-doc, John Coupland, we established pretty soon what I had to focus on. John was such a great help. Before he got involved, I had been totally lost. Having come from engineering, working in a wet lab was new to me, and I had to learn fast. During the experimental phase of the PhD, I planned the protocol and stuck to the schedule diligently, inputting my results every day and analysing data as early as I could.

I was in a serious relationship around this time too. We seemed to have a lot in common. I liked facts and he liked facts. He loved his job and I really admired that about him. I loved to see how passionate he was about his work, particularly as I enjoyed working hard too.

I also made lasting friendships during my PhD, which was fortunate, as my friends kept me sane during that time, particularly during the write-up phase of my thesis. Michael, in particular, was my true pal. He and I sat opposite each other in our lab and we had tons in common, especially a wicked sense of humour. Michael has this astute awareness of people and cares deeply for his friends. He's still my best friend, which likely has a lot to do with that shared experience of completing our PhDs together.

Writing up my thesis was extremely challenging for me. While my experimental phase went really well, my write-up phase was a nightmare. Maybe it was because of my inexperience in writing for science publications, or maybe every PhD candidate feels the way I did, but completing my PhD was without doubt the most difficult thing I have ever done. It nearly broke me: the sense of powerlessness and isolation was very intense. I saw other colleagues suffering;

some walked away because they had to, others had to be medicated to get through it. We all coped in our own way.

Completing my PhD came at a cost. Spending all that time in isolation, in thought, there could be no other distractions. The relationship with my partner broke down six months shy of my submission date, not because of the thesis, but because of the circumstances I put myself in. He was a lovely person and took very good care of me at the time. But the PhD came first above all else and our relationship was a casualty of that commitment. I gave everything to the completion of my thesis and got completely absorbed in that world. Nothing else mattered.

I felt that if I could just complete my thesis then I could move on to the next phase of my life. I would succeed. The pressure that I put on myself to meet the Christmas 1999 deadline was extreme. My three supervisors didn't think that I could finish on time; it was a race to the end, lots of arguments, tears and exhaustion. I had a post-doctoral position starting in early January. I had to make this deadline. Finally, my supervisors relented and I managed to get the thesis in on time.

I don't think that my thesis was exceptional; even after all that work and commitment, all I could produce was a pretty average study. After all the years I gave to my PhD, all the hope and pride that I'd felt as I began the process, I was disappointed in myself with the final outcome. So while my parents and people outside the academic community were lauding me, I really wasn't comfortable with any of it. I was proud of the achievement, and that I had survived the process, but no matter how much I loved science, I knew that I was always going to be an average researcher and academic.

***

In hindsight, the post-doc position in the food technology department in UCC was doomed from the start. I was going through a lot. Between processing the relationship failure and recovering from the PhD, I couldn't settle. I hadn't given myself any time off to really deal with the massive upheaval that had occurred in my life. I thought that if I kept busy I could make it go away. But, of course, I couldn't. Something had to change.

I was also starting to realise that a career in academia would never be enough for me. I loved the scientific process, I loved figuring things out, I loved working with other postgrads, supervising their projects, but the environment just didn't work for me. I would never be happy there.

Thinking that a change of scenery would do the trick, I applied for a research position in Nelson, New Zealand, at Crop & Food Research on a project making edible films from fish skins. I had a two-hour phone interview with T. C. Chadderton, the head of the department. Then they invited me for a two-week visit to have another interview and check out the area. So in July 2002, I flew to Nelson. And it was stunning. It's a small, quiet town at the top of the South Island, in the heart of wine country and nestled between two national parks. The job had a lot of potential benefits. I had always wanted to live self-sufficiently and this environment would allow me to explore buying my own plot. Part of my role would also involve travelling to the Antarctic to collect fish samples.

Before I returned home, T. C. offered me the job. The University of Canterbury also got wind of my visit to New Zealand and flew me down to Christchurch; they even had a special reception in my honour. I was given a tour of their food science department. I was offered a job as a lecturer and researcher on the spot. It all felt too good to be true. Back in Ireland, I had a mediocre PhD and was dying slowly in my post-doc position. I returned home and told everyone about the opportunity, proud of myself for the first time in years. Mam and Dad seemed proud, though my sister, Deirdre, told me that they were worried about me. Still, I accepted the position with Crop & Food officially about a week after returning home.

In September, I went to London to collect my visa from the New Zealand embassy. Crown Relocations came to visit Mull's Cottage to provide a quote for my relocation. It would all be covered in my contract, as well as return flights home every year for the first two years. This was a good deal. It seemed like the opportunity that I had always wanted. I handed in my notice to my supervisor at UCC. He was delighted and quick to congratulate me; this would be an opportunity for us to collaborate together internationally. I would begin on 10 January 2003.

This was it, I kept telling myself; this was the change that I needed to get me out of my haze. I really was looking forward to living in such a stunning country. But something was off. Still, on the outside, I was smiling.

During this post-doc period I had returned to acting after a six-year hiatus. The Granary Theatre in Cork attracted professional, student and amateur shows. I auditioned for a role in Caryl Churchill's *Cloud Nine*, got the part and pretty soon I was getting cast in a lot more shows. And I loved it. It was a big highlight of my time at UCC. I loved hanging out with these creatives; everyone was so open and passionate and playful. I enjoy the process of putting on a play: the rehearsals, the technical elements and the run itself. All these different phases have their own pressures, but when you're in a good show and surrounded by a great team, each is very rewarding.

After handing in my notice, I took holidays from work and went up to Dundalk to spend time with Mam and Dad. And I signed up for a one-week acting class at the Gaiety School of Acting. As the time for my New Zealand move approached, the whole thing felt more and more like the wrong move. Eventually, I had to act.

In November, I rang T. C. and declined the job offer. Mam and Dad were so relieved when I told them. They had been worried about me heading off to a strange country on my own. It turned out that they were aware of this need within me to be creative. Knowing that they loved me and that I had their support no matter what I chose to do with my life was huge for me.

I hadn't a clue what I was doing. But it felt like I was

heading in the right direction, particularly when I finally accepted that I didn't want to continue working in academia. It was time to make a big choice. Time to try something completely new and see how it felt. Time to start properly exploring my creative side.

I was back behind the steering wheel of my life. For the first time in ten years, I felt that passion stir. Even though I was walking away from a career that I had devoted nearly fourteen years of my life to create, I finally felt successful in that moment.

Dundalk
2002
Dad's shed
Aviary
Budgies, twenty-four-to-sixty-five
Quails, reproducing rapidly
Cupboards, shelves, flip chart, printer, computers
Mess!

Man, sixty-three
Grey
White shirt
Rolled-up sleeves
Vest
Cream slacks
Farah.

Girl – woman, thirty-three
Red hair

Long
Pale
Thin
Too thin
She's here on a week's holiday to Dundalk.

She works in a lab
in Cork
She lives alone
She has one friend.

Dad: Right now Niamh, we're going to do a five-year plan for you.
Because if you don't have a plan,
you don't know where you're going.
And we're going to write it all down on this flip chart here.
So first question is 'Who are you?'

Niamh: I don't know.

Dad: Okay, let me ask you another way, 'What do you want to be?'

Niamh: I can't say it.

Dad: Why not?

Niamh: All those years, the research, the work, fourteen years.

Dad: Don't worry about that, the great thing about education is that you will always have it, and you'll find a way of using it. So forget that for now.

So what do you want to be?

Niamh: I can't say it.

Dad: You can!

Dad: Alright, I'll say it for you.
I am an …
Say it, Niamh.

Dad: I am an …

Dad: … ACTOR

A screen behind Niamh projects 'Astronaut'

Dad: Cos that's what you are.
Isn't that right, Niamh?
An Actor?

– Excerpt from *To Space*, 2014

Chapter 4

The Actor and Failing

From January 2003 I was formally an actor. I got my head-shots, took regular acting classes, approached casting directors to introduce myself and finally landed an agent. In a matter of months, I was all set. I became a member of an improvisation comedy troupe, Snatch Comedy, while in Cork and the change of career was a breath of fresh air.

I took up yoga and exercise and started to take really good care of myself. Because, before I left my job in academia, I really hadn't been in a good place. I felt broken, my passion for science all but gone. Physically and mentally I had still been burnt-out from the PhD.

I realised that it was time for a fresh start. That's why, in August 2003, I decided to leave Cork and move to Dublin. It was tough, because I loved Cork. I had found this beautiful home, I had my improv troupe, and I was acting regularly. My best pal, Michael, was living there too. I felt reluctant to uproot everything and start again. But Dublin ended up being a really good decision.

On my first weekend in the city, I went to see another improv comedy troupe, The Bankers Comedy Improv, to see if they were looking for new members. Their show was good; some were strong improvisers. They had a regular venue at

The Bankers Bar, performing every Friday.

I really loved improvisation and had taken to it quickly. I had been a big fan of Channel 4's *Whose Line is it Anyway?* and my brother John and I had been improvising sketches at home for years, making tapes together, honing our own humour style. I had done well with my Snatch Comedy troupe in Cork, and really enjoyed our gigs. I mean, I had been terrified and some of the early gigs were really tough, but I still loved it. Allowing yourself to be inspired in the moment, the sensation of being in the moment, the lack of control – it had all felt new to me. I had always been in control before: in work, in my personal life, and even in my acting. This was completely different and I soon realised that the more open and engaged I was, while listening to my improv partners, the better a performer I became. I would be astounded by my imagination and how a scene would just come together by working with my partner. I would always be terrified at the start of the night, but it was always worth it.

Improv also helped me to genuinely open up more to audiences; to lose my mask of performance altogether; to be completely present and exposed and vulnerable with them. It was terrifying initially, but after slowly adjusting myself year after year, I got there. You have to acknowledge the audience in the show. In improv shows you need them with you at all times as they are the people feeding you the set-up ideas for each game or scene. I figured out pretty quickly that the more I connected with the audience, even just by having banter with them at intervals or between games, the more relaxed I became.

I drove up and down to Cork every Monday during my first year in Dublin, meaning I got to continue working with Snatch, as well as becoming a core member of The Bankers, which is where I met Peter, the gentlest, warmest and most sincere person I think I have ever had the privilege to love.

I'm not sure if I would be on this path to space if it weren't for Peter. He was patient and kind and took great care of me, something that I really needed. And he loved me unconditionally. No matter what I did, or said, he never left. Sure, we had rows and disagreements, especially in the early days when I was particularly defensive, but I always knew that he wouldn't leave. He showed me a lot and helped me open my heart in a way that I hadn't really known. He brought out the warm, caring and kind part of me and showed me how much there is to gain by loving unconditionally. And he trusted me. My opinion of the world changed a lot because of Peter. I owe him a great deal.

I was afforded an opportunity to study film acting in Los Angeles in 2006, which took me away for two months. I really wanted to do it but was sure that Peter probably wouldn't be comfortable with us being apart for that length of time. However, no, that wasn't the case at all. He couldn't have been more encouraging. We didn't have much money, with us both being actors, but every penny he earned was mine. And vice versa. So we made it work, we figured out the finances and I went to LA to study film acting. And improv too. I took classes at the illustrious The Second City and performed with them every Saturday night in their midnight show, which was an improv jam. Again, I was terrified to be performing with such experienced players, but I held my own. I felt I was becoming a better actor and performer.

***

While I was in LA, I was called to audition for a role in *Fair City*. Since I was not in Dublin, I was gutted that I was going to miss the opportunity. Thankfully, my acting coach suggested that I tape my audition and send it to them. This is a common method of auditioning now – you can audition for roles all over the world thanks to Skype and our smartphones, but in 2006 it was a lot trickier. Videotape was the only method of doing that. So I worked with my coach and I put down all the required scenes, probably much better than I would ever have done in Dublin without her assistance. I didn't get that particular role, but about eight months later I got offered the part of Sr Frances McGuigan off the back of that tape.

Fair City was a part of my life for about a year from 2007 to 2008. In the soap opera, I played a nun who returns home from the missions in the Democratic Republic of the Congo for her sister Tracey's wedding. As with all characters on the show, nothing was as it seemed. I had left the order because I was suffering from post-traumatic stress disorder (as you do) after witnessing the murder of members of a family whom I had been particularly close to in my diocese. After that story unravelled, I got work in the Bistro, started dating a fridge repair guy, whom I subsequently got engaged to and lost my virginity to, only for him to then admit that he frequented brothels. This sent me into a tailspin, so I went to speak about it with my sister, who then admitted that she was once a prostitute to feed her heroin habit. That was all too much to deal with, so I ran back to the convent and was last seen hugging my sister and then being whisked off in a taxi (the ultimate death of a character in *Fair City*), never to return.

I know that soaps get a lot of flack, and that some people suggest the quality isn't the best, but having been on the other side of the lens, I can't help but admire how this machine involving so many elements and people manages to get four episodes out every week. From the writers, set design, lighting, sound, camera crew, wardrobe, make-up, floor crew, directors, producers and actors, it's a juggernaut of a show. The days are very long and if your storyline is the focus of a run of episodes you can shoot, on average, about seventeen scenes a day. You really have to be on top of your game and there is no time to commit to anything else.

I hadn't realised what a huge undertaking the show would be. The schedule was brutal and even on the days that I would have only a few scenes to shoot, I was still learning lines or doing costume fittings or hanging around on set, waiting for my scene to be shot. Everyone gets to know each other very quickly, as we're all working together in bringing our best to each element of the show. I learned a great deal in those ten months as Sr Frances, and made lasting friendships too.

I was delighted to have been a part of the show, and it helped that it was the first time that I obtained a fairly decent wage as an actor. My parents were absolutely thrilled for me; to them, this was pretty much the pinnacle of an actor's career. I hadn't realised the huge following that the show had. Getting recognised everywhere that I went was very strange, and not something that I ever got used to. Even now, well over a decade on from that fateful taxi, people will still approach me and ask me about *Fair City*.

***

I had a respectable career as an actor, performing in a number of theatre shows, touring across Ireland, as well as picking up a number of small screen roles in UK shows that were shooting in Ireland. It's all summarised on the IMDb website if you're interested.

The biggest screen opportunity that came my way was probably an audition for the movie *Albert Nobbs*, starring Glenn Close, in 2010. I progressed through a number of callbacks, eventually reading against Ms Close herself. The callbacks were held in a disused office block in Sandyford Industrial Estate. I arrived about an hour early because I was terrified that I would get stuck in traffic en route. All the sitting and waiting made me more nervous and so by the time the audition came around I had completely freaked myself out. Glenn Close! I mean, she was in *Fatal Attraction*.

The room was tiny. Sitting across from me were the director, three producers and then, slightly obscured by a big light and sitting facing the wall, Ms Close herself. She remained quiet and very understated throughout the process; it was difficult to know what she was thinking.

My first read seemed fine to me; the director was happy with it, as were all the producers. They thought that I looked perfect for the role as a maid. (Can I just say that nearly all my screen roles were as nuns, nurses or maids!) Then everyone looked to Glenn for her comments. She liked it too but said, smiling throughout, that she would be 'curious to see what it might be like if I did it again, but this time, a little more soft-spoken, more quietly'.

Delighted to get feedback, I jumped straight back in. Again the director was happy, but again Glenn asked me to do it another time, but even more quietly. So I did. And again, after that take, I was asked to do it more quietly. So now all I'm thinking about is how to be that quiet! I could barely even hear myself say the words at this stage, I was almost just mouthing them.

Scene ended. Silence. Everyone looked to Glenn, and she looked at me, pointing at me, saying, 'And there she is!' The director agreed enthusiastically, as did all the producers, congratulating me on such 'great work – so insightful to the character'. There was a lot of handshaking and in seconds I was on the other side of the room. I was baffled as to how that last read could possibly have been as profoundly brilliant as they had all told me.

My agent called me that afternoon. Despite the glowing reaction, I didn't get the part. I wasn't a big enough name. Maria Doyle Kennedy got my part in the end.

***

The lack of control over my acting career was a big challenge for me. It was beginning to wear on me and, as much as I loved performing, I wasn't sure if I was cut out for a life of, well, waiting and hoping for my big break. Still, throughout all those years of acting, even in the quiet times, there was always The Bankers improv troupe and our Friday night show in the basement of The Bankers Bar on Dame Lane. (We renamed ourselves The Craic Pack some time around 2005.)

I had also begun working with University College Dublin (UCD) and its science department on providing communications workshops for postgrads and post-docs through using improvisation and theatre skills. Working with Patrick Sutton, director of the Gaiety School of Acting, we put together a curriculum to assist the academic community in their presentation skills, and called it 'Straight Talking Science'. Leaning on those years of improvising with The Craic Pack, Snatch Comedy and Second City, we used play, body language and spontaneity to bring their research alive.

We discovered that the actor Alan Alda had also realised the power of improvisation in simplifying dense science jargon for academics. Alda is a successful American actor who is probably best known for his role as Hawkeye in *M*A*S*H* and as Arnold Vinick in *The West Wing*. While he was making a TV show with *Scientific American*, he found that scientists relaxed more after a session of improvisation; they were more present, more charismatic and communicated much more clearly. He then set up the Alda Centre for Communicating Science in Stony Brook, New York. We reached out to him to tell him that we had stumbled upon the same phenomenon, and he applauded what we were doing, sharing his thoughts in a lovely article in *The Irish Times*. Our workshop was a great success. It showed me that improv was a valuable tool in my arsenal.

I think improv has not only made me a better communicator, it has also affected the way I see the world. The basic principles of improvisation demand that you open your heart. Having to say 'Yes, and' to every single opportunity with my partner on stage, accepting every suggestion that I'm given in order to build a scene and create something together. Believing in this and trusting it every time I got on stage has made me fearless in my choices in scenes.

I learned a lot about performing with The Craic Pack improv troupe. Perhaps the three biggest things that I learned were, first, to let go and trust my team, that they had my back. Secondly, I learned not to be afraid of failing but instead to celebrate it. We often had better shows when things went wrong. And thirdly, I learned so much about connecting with audiences. For example, how the more present and relaxed I was during my performance, the more they then relaxed and were willing to come with me on my journey.

Thanks to acting and performing, I changed my relationship and understanding of failure. As someone who came from an academic background, always striving for excellence, failure was a bad thing. But how can failure be bad? How can we possibly improve if we don't learn, and learning requires a capacity to fail. I learned to ride a bicycle by falling a lot.

Failing is a natural part of learning when we're very young, and then school comes along and from that point on failure is perceived as a bad thing. But the definition of failure in the Oxford dictionary is 'the absence of success'. So failure and success are tied together. Based on that definition, I began to see failure and success as two ends of a scale, where failure was at one side and success at the other. So if I tried at all, then I had to be moving along that scale, moving closer towards success. Failure is standing still. Failure is not trying. Failure is being gripped with fear, leaving you incapacitated to even try. And so, conversely, any attempt to confront that fear is a success.

I discussed improvisation and how that helped me reshape my perceptions of success and failure in a TEDx talk I gave at UCD in 2014.

I began to see that for the past thirty-plus years, I had been standing still. I was too afraid to even try to live the life that I wanted. Once I figured that out, things started changing.

Rapidly.

What was my definition of success? This was something that I hadn't given much consideration to during all those years of my academic career. I had just assumed that I was succeeding based on the behaviour of people around me. I hadn't really thought about what I personally considered to be success. And once I started looking at this, I finally understood that I was miserable because I was living a life based on other people's perceptions of success. Not my own definition of success.

So what is success to me?

Success, to me, is staying curious, making a difference, and feeling that my life has meaning. Success is being surrounded by love and happiness, creativity, facts, information, a lifetime of learning. And being able to go to bed at the end of the day knowing that I haven't intentionally offended anyone. Success is a clear conscience, a life of self-development and a contribution to the world that will yield a positive outcome.

And once I knew that, I could finally make peace with all the decisions that I had made in my life, and with the fact that somewhere along the way, probably in my teens, I had forgotten what I wanted to be and begun to live a life that matched a successful life based on everyone else's perceptions of success rather than my own. While I'm very proud to have my degrees in engineering and science, and proud to have had a worthy career in acting, they weren't quite my complete definition of success. Others valued those achievements more than I did. Something was missing in all of it for me. But now I was done with that.

I realised that, deep down, there was a part of me that still held on to what I truly felt would be a success for me. The same part of myself that made me walk away from so many opportunities or relationships in the past. That's why I stepped away from academia, that's why I became an actor – or, more importantly, a creative. I was nudging myself towards my true goal. But I wasn't quite there yet. And by no longer being afraid of failing, and realising that I had the capability to define my own measure of success, I was finally available to begin that journey of discovery.

And it no longer needed to make sense to anyone else. As long as it made sense to me, as long as I knew in my gut that I was on the right track, that would be enough. I had finally found my path, my route to personal success. I was on the scale, no longer standing still. The sense of relief, the lightness that it brought to my life, was extraordinary. Truly knowing and accepting that I could do whatever I liked with my life was exciting. That there were no boundaries, except those that I set myself. I was so very happy, truly happy, for the first time in years.

It was time to find a way to bring it all together.

Chapter 5

The Science Communicator

I slowly started to bring science back into my life. It started to become natural to me to explain science in an everyday way, which seemed to appeal to people who hadn't studied science. I did a lot of reading about careers that combine science and creativity and found out about 'science communication'.

Then I found Mary Mulvihill and contacted her to ask her a few questions about what she did. A scientist, radio broadcaster, author and educator, she founded and served as the first chairperson of Women in Technology and Science, and is viewed as a pioneer of science communication in Ireland. A really lovely person too, she paved the way for many of us in helping to carve out a career in science communication. (She sadly passed away far too soon in 2015. She is sorely missed and I owe her a great debt of gratitude.) She very kindly took my call and explained all about this new world that I knew nothing about, where writers and journalists specialised in communicating science to a general audience, sharing new research and discoveries. She told me about a course at DCU in communications that specialised in this field (linking back to my CAO form and my applying for communications all those years ago).

I wanted to be a part of it, so I contacted Brian Trench,

who was then course director of the Masters degree in science communications – another person whom I admire and respect and who has also contributed a great deal to the science sector. We agreed that the course would be of huge benefit to what I was trying to do. I wasn't necessarily interested in becoming a journalist, but there was a lot in the course that appealed to my quest to combine science with creativity in some way. I could do the Masters part-time too, over two years, so it was perfect. With my qualifications, I met the criteria for application and so I proceeded. Then I got a huge bill for fees that was about four times more expensive than I had seen on some site. I didn't have the money. I chatted about it with Brian; we were both disappointed, but he advised me to try entering the field anyway. The Masters would have been hugely beneficial, sure, but I didn't really need a qualification to explore that middle ground.

Just try? I figured that he was right. I had to just try and see what happened.

Through the improv, people had been inviting me on radio for panel shows for quite a while, usually to be the funny girl on the panel. It immediately came easy to me: to chat, to be relaxed and so I got invited on air a lot, especially at Newstalk. Once I figured out that I wanted to try bringing more science to the radio, I contacted different shows, pitching the idea to them. Soon I was appearing on TV and on radio shows such as *The John Murray Show* and *The Dave Fanning Show* on RTÉ, among others, as a science communicator/presenter. I also became resident scientist on Gráinne and Síle Seoige's daytime TV show on RTÉ. My new career in science communication had begun in earnest.

***

But while presenting scientific topics to the general public is something that I really enjoy, I prefer presenting a sort of thesis or idea – particularly when I get to present it in a creative way. With this in mind, I began to work with an experimental theatre company, ANU Productions. They were a progressive team of artists, visual artists and actors, led by the accomplished director Louise Lowe and visual artist Owen Boss. Their work was devised and then presented in a non-theatre setting. It broke the rules of conventional theatre. They particularly liked the fact that I was curious about incorporating science into performances and encouraged me all the time to contribute to the rehearsal room. I owe them a great deal for encouraging this in me.

As the company succeeded, winning awards for their shows, being attached to that success meant that I was taken seriously as this creative who brought science to theatre. And I got a chance to make my first show. Again, gripped by fear, I began to piece it together. My colleague from ANU Productions, Una, kindly accepted my invitation for her to direct, although she became more than a director; she became my dramaturge too. She made me feel safe to keep exploring; safe to stop worrying about the final version and just keep looking.

I was also very lucky to obtain support from Arts@CERN

to come visit the facility in Switzerland in preparation for my show, which I was calling *That's About the Size of It*.

I also received a bursary for a residency at the Tyrone Guthrie Centre as part of a theatre-making initiative called MAKE, as well as a spot in the 'Show in a Bag' scheme, which afforded me an opportunity to perform the show in Bewleys Theatre as part of Dublin Fringe Festival 2011. It was the first time that I had ever made theatre on my own, let alone combining it with science themes. I was terrified that I wasn't going to pull it off.

I had this one, big, still-quite-vague idea that I had been mulling over for about a year, and even though I was terrified, I still wanted to see it through. It felt as if something was bubbling up inside me and if I didn't get it out I was going to explode. I wasn't entirely sure what that 'something' was, but it was starting to come into focus, and it had something to do with my place in the very big and the very small. I was trying to figure out my place in the story of the universe, in terms of the scale and where I stood on that scale. And while I had read about the Big Bang, the planets and the stars, I still didn't feel a part of anything beyond Earth. I wanted to explore that idea further, so instead of thinking about the very big elements that make up our universe, I thought about the very small ones, and wondered if there was somehow a connection or similarity in behaviour between the very big and the very small. And so I naturally arrived at atoms.

During my research, I read about the Higgs boson, which at that time had yet to be measured. (In the 1960s Peter Higgs was among several physicists who proposed a mechanism to explain why the most fundamental building blocks of the universe have mass. The mechanism predicted a particle – the Higgs boson, which soon became known as the 'God particle' – that could help us better understand the physical forces that make up our universe. On 4 July 2012 scientists at CERN tentatively confirmed that they had found a Higgs particle.) As part of my trip to CERN, I met with theoretical and experimental particle physicists to ensure that I understood the overarching principles of their work to discover the Higgs boson, and the relevance of concepts such as the standard equation, super-symmetry and string theory in explaining the origins of our universe and the behaviour of matter. I found that these theories were extraordinarily beautiful and philosophical. And creative too.

I looked at string theory in particular and its underlying principles, and it struck a chord in helping me make sense of things. It changed the way I saw myself, my perception of myself, in the overall scheme of things.

Here's an excerpt from that show to explain further:

> *One thing I did discover at CERN is that the physicists there are trying to figure out one clear, succinct equation*

that would describe the whole universe – A Theory of
Everything.

The Standard Model can only account for the behaviour of
things at the atomic level. Einstein's Theory of Relativity
makes sense only for very heavy matter, such as the
planets, solar systems and galaxies.

Is there a theory that can explain everything, from the
smallest infinitesimal thing to the universe itself?
There is, or at least there could be – and it comes from a
theory called string theory!

String theory says that the particles making up everything
in the universe are made up of
even smaller ingredients, tiny wiggling strands of energy
that look a lot like strings.
Each of these strings is unimaginably small and exists in
a higher dimension.
The tenth dimension.
In fact, if an atom were enlarged to the size of the solar
system, a string would only be as large as a tree on our
planet.
This means that, right now, the atoms that make up who I
am, who you are, are composed
of vibrating strings of energy and we are therefore all
existing in the tenth dimension.

I exist on the tenth dimension?
I thought that I existed just on the third dimension, but
no, now I'm on the tenth!

– Excerpt from *That's About the Size of It*, 2011

In exploring string theory, I happened upon this notion that quite possibly everything that makes up who I am – in fact, everything around us, from the smallest to the biggest things in our universe – is composed of vibrating strings of energy that are so unimaginably small they can only be described as existing on the tenth dimension.

Allow me to briefly review dimensions with you. As far as my limited understanding goes, we exist right now in a world that appears to be three dimensional, the third dimension. That is because we can describe everything in three ways: length, depth and height. The second dimension, in contrast, describes objects in two dimensions: height and length (like a square on a page). And the first dimension would be one point on that square, i.e. it would account for only one of those dimensions. On the other hand, it is possible to describe more and more complex systems as you increase the number of dimensions. For example, the fourth dimension generally accounts for length, height, depth and duration. The fifth accounts for different probable outcomes of that fourth dimension. And on and on, adding more and more complexity to the measurements, until we arrive at the tenth dimension, which can theoretically account for all futures, all pasts, all beginnings and all ends, infinitely extended. Basically, it's a dimension of anything you can imagine.

Like I said earlier, I had limited mathematical capability and found this concept very difficult to grasp at times, but the general notion of it struck a chord with me. And I was interested in exploring artistically that notion that somehow we could all exist on the tenth dimension. And if we look at what that means, it told me that every possible permutation and combination of all my life choices has been calculated and all the possible outcomes of my life are existing right now in these higher dimensions. I happen to be on one course, but there are many, many different outcomes of my life, your life, our universe happening right now on these higher dimensions.

That thought set me free. To me, it meant that every conceivable outcome of my life was in fact possible and if I could somehow gain an ability to perceive these higher dimensions, I could look down on my life and all the different paths and choices I may or may not have taken. And I could see them all and simply activate the life that I truly want. I had found a way to change my perception of my life. Looking at my life, looking down on it. I had found my own overview.

This thesis – to view the possible lives that I wanted to reflect on – became the central premise for my performance. I wanted to share them with the audience and, using video, portray myself as if I existed in each of these concurrent lives. By doing this, I could be the ballerina or the astronaut that I dreamed of being as a child, or be a wife and mother, or be an artist or the scientist in the lab or the girl who emigrated to New Zealand. To complete the thesis, all we had to do was create a video for each of these concurrent lives. As the rehearsals continued, we set about creating those videos. And that's when everything changed forever.

> *We are all made of atoms.*
> *And speaking of atoms,*
> *did you know that the electrons that spin around the atoms*
> *that make up your body interact with electrons from other*
> *objects too?*
> *For instance, as you sit on that chair, the electrons from*
> *your hands and your 'behind' or 'derriere' are actually inter-*
> *acting with the electrons from the chair.*
> *Such that, when you get up and leave this show, you have*
> *left a little part of your 'behind' behind.*
> *Here, in this room.*
> *Which has now become part of that chair.*
>
> *And that chair has also given you a little part of themselves*
> *too.*
> *Same with people you shake hands with. Embrace. Hold.*
> *I like that.*
> *To think that everything and everyone is connected.*

CUE: Astronaut Niamh video

> *Astronaut me! My Astronaut Niamh. 'What If!'*
> *Ah, I love her!*
> *She's very close.*
> *She could be right beside me, right now.*
> *But I can see her now, from the tenth dimension. She*
> *wants to be an astronaut.*
> *She split from me very young.*

*Aged seven–eight. She's been on this path since then. She
still wants it. She still wants it.*

If I could grab her and jump into her life, I would.

*When I go there in my mind and imagine and dream that
world of astronauts and stations,*

*adventures and new frontiers, I stay there for a long time,
basking in it.*

*Look at her – in a Russian capsule for orbital re-entry at
the International Space University in Strasbourg on Yuri's
night last week.*

*Meeting top NASA and ESA experts and discussing their
twenty-year plans for a manned mission to Mars.*

*She makes me feel that anything is possible, that I can
dream anything, be anything I want to be.*

I want to know if she made it to space.

I think I'll ask her.

*Because, in the fourth dimension, we see three-dimensional
objects like a long undulating worm, which encapsulates
every moment in our lives as a long series of slices of
moments – from the moment of birth to the moment of
death.*

*And in the third dimension, I can only see my life, one slice
at a time.*

*But in higher dimensions, the tenth dimension, I can see
the worms of all my parallel
universes from beginning to end.*

*So, there's nothing stopping me looking at her, at a different
slice of her life, not today, but further on down the line.*

CUE: Future Astronaut Niamh video (played by my mother)

In thirty years' time.
2043.
In fact, I think I will.
Here she is. Obviously the decor of kitchens hasn't changed much in thirty years!
I have to know. I have to ask her.
'And did you go to space?'

Future Astronaut Niamh replies 'Yes.' She then takes us to her keyboard and plays music, occasionally peeking up at the camera to ensure that we're still watching her.

She did!
She went to space.
She was right to hold on to her dreams.

All matter is made up of atoms.
And now I know that all matter is composed of these vibrating strings of energy.
Which means that if I can understand that and harness that, then I can become whatever I want to be.

There's nothing stopping me morphing into something else.
I already leave my electrons everywhere I go in the third dimension.
So in the tenth dimension, I could morph into a chair or I could morph into a television, or a bird, or a carpet, or air –
ANYTHING!
Into anything I want to be.

– Excerpt from *That's About the Size of It*, 2011

Chapter 6

The Moment of Clarity

In August 2011 I got in touch with the European Space Agency head office in Paris. I spoke with Clare Mattok in their communications office and asked her if I could borrow one of their astronaut flight suits for my play because I wanted to create a parallel life where I achieve my ultimate dream and become an astronaut. She was keen to help me and sent me a flight suit on the proviso that I return it within the month. I gratefully accepted her kind offer and thanked her profusely. I couldn't believe how easy it was to get hold of an astronaut's flight suit. Why hadn't I done anything like this before?

So we began shooting the 'Astronaut Niamh' video for the show. All the others were in the can by this stage, with the show opening in less than three weeks. I had left this one till last. I think it was because I was really struggling with how to create this parallel life, this 'Astronaut Niamh' version of myself. I had nothing in my current life that linked to it. I somehow hadn't even taken up an astronomy course. A set of binoculars and the names of a few constellations were the only leftovers I had of my childhood dream.

I felt a bit silly. Maybe it wasn't true; maybe I had imagined that this had been my dream when I was a kid. I knew that I had often told people that I had wanted to be an astronaut when I was trying to impress them, but other than that, where was the evidence? I starting thinking that maybe we shouldn't use this 'Astronaut Niamh' in the show; maybe I was forcing it?

In the end, I was forced to fall back on the TV shows that I watched as a child; the ones that had fed that excitement about becoming an astronaut: *The Six Million Dollar Man, Blake's 7, Doctor Who, Star Trek, Star Wars, Space 1999, The Gemini Man*, the 'Slimey to the Moon' scene from *Sesame Street,* and more. I lined them up to watch on YouTube.

Once everything was prepared, I set up my laptop and took out the flight suit. It was a few sizes too big for me, but it was still awesome to have it in my hands! I noticed that there were Velcro sections on it to display your name. And the official ESA badge was on it too. However, when I put it on, it immediately felt very odd; it didn't seem right. I felt deeply uncomfortable sitting on the couch in front of the laptop with the flight suit on. This wasn't my suit to wear, I thought; I haven't earned this. This was created for someone who worked very hard to become an astronaut. What was supposed to be a light-hearted video for the show was slowly becoming something very unsettling for me.

We began recording. I was smiling, watching *The Six Million Dollar Man*, though I was starting to feel deeply uncomfortable and very self-aware. The next video came on; it was Tony Bennett on *Sesame Street* with Big Bird, singing 'Slimey to the Moon'. It's in the episode where Big Bird's friend, Slimey the worm, launches to the Moon in his tiny spacecraft. I love this show and this particular episode. But watching it in that moment, wearing the ESA flight suit, made me feel sad. It was a deep sadness, something that had crept up on me really fast and so I began to cry. I wasn't playing any more for the camera; I just started to focus on watching the clip, deeply aware that I was in an astronaut's flight suit that wasn't mine. I was ashamed of myself because I felt like I was mocking this dream that I once had, one that I realised in that moment was still very real.

For all my talk of once wanting to be an astronaut, for all my passion for space, what had I actually done to achieve my dream over the years? When I was in Florida, back in 1989, on a college holiday, I didn't even visit the Kennedy Space Center. I'd never written to an astronaut or anyone remotely related to space. I'd never met anyone involved in the space industry. Other than Dad's *National Geographic* pull-out posters, like that *Earthrise* picture, and what I read as a kid in the encyclopaedia, I'd never tried to really learn about space, never mind get there. And as I sat on the couch, I was mortified to be in that flight suit, because it wasn't mine and I realised there and then that it would never be mine. Ever.

My reflections in that moment were, thankfully, caught on tape.

Sitting there, everything came together: the wasted years, why I had felt so lost, why I had struggled to commit to any career. I was a fake, a big fat fake. And sitting in that flight suit, I felt the embarrassment of my existence, the years of avoidance, of being afraid to be the one person I knew deep down I had always wanted to be.

I knew who I was at eight years of age, but I had been too scared to even try to fulfil a tiny part of who I really wanted to be. I had bailed on myself. I didn't even try. How could I possibly have let that happen? Was I lacking that much self-belief or confidence? Or was it more that I had worried too much about what people would say? Or was I simply too lazy to grab life and live it to its maximum?

***

Everything changed that day. I knew that if I didn't do anything about facing my dream I would be haunted for the rest of my life. I had to confront it. I had no choice.

I really believe that in making *That's About the Size of It*, by exploring that notion of our place in and the scale of the universe, I had somehow activated 'Astronaut Niamh'. By observing it, bearing witness, it felt as if I jumped into one of the other possible outcomes of my life. I finally made the leap back to the life that my eight-year-old self always wanted.

The show went up during the Dublin Fringe Festival that September. It did okay and was well received by audiences, especially the science community. It was by no means perfect; it was my first show, after all. But people liked the ideas that were explored, and were thankful to have a better grasp of the work taking place at CERN too. They were delighted that they understood this complex science a little better.

I learned a huge amount from making the show, personally and professionally. And I slowly started finding new avenues for bringing space-related activities into my life.

But nothing happens overnight.

I had recently joined Twitter and was following a few science people but no one from the space community. Social media was an easy way to start exploring this area, so I started with the NASA and ESA accounts. 'Tweet ups' had become a thing around then – an opportunity for Twitterers to attend promotional events for organisations, i.e. basically an opportunity for them to get free press. I applied to NASA for some tweet ups to attend launches in Florida but was never successful. The same went for ESA. Eventually, I came across another tweet up to mark Yuri's Night (which occurs annually on 12 April, celebrating Yuri Gagarin's achievement on that day back in 1961 in being the first person in space). This time I got the invite.

The tweet-up event took place at the International Space University (ISU) in Strasbourg in conjunction with a two-day conference about Mars. The Twitterers had their own schedule of activities, like a live link-up with Bill Nye; a talk from Diego Urbina, who, in 2010, had participated in a simulated Mars mission called Mars500 for 520 days with a crew of five others (including Romain Charles from ESA); and a talk from the course director, Angie Bukley, of the Space Studies Program.

She was on secondment (a temporary transfer) from NASA to plan this nine-week intensive residential programme that would cover all aspects of space, including the humanities. It attracted over 120 participants from all over the world and was taught by leading experts covering all fields of space science and engineering. Some of the other Twitterers were applying for the programme. I wanted to go so badly, but there was no way that I could afford the exorbitant fees. And there was also Peter to consider.

That first day in Strasbourg, I also met Chris Welch, director of the Masters programme at ISU, for the first time. He was someone who had a keen interest in artists exploring space themes. As part of the tweet up event, I also got to spend time in the orbital module of a Soyuz spacecraft (part of the spacecraft used to bring astronauts to the International Space Station). We celebrated Yuri's Night that evening with vodka and a lecture from Pete Worden, who at the time was director of the NASA Ames Research Center.

On the second day, I sat in on the Mars conference and was astounded by the papers that were being presented: urine purification systems for human missions, and spacecraft design for return missions to the Moon and Mars. In mere months since my epiphany, my whole life had turned around. By simply reaching out via Twitter, I was at a conference about human missions to Mars and the Moon. It had been this close to me all along; all I had to do was apply for a tweet up. I just never had the courage to seek it out before.

Shortly after Strasbourg, I received funding from Dublin

City of Science to bring my show to the Project Arts Centre. We had a chance to adjust some elements of the show, so I brought in some video of that trip to ISU. 'Astronaut Niamh' was now a part of my current life, no longer a possible outcome. We also brought the show to CIT Blackrock Castle Observatory as part of the Cork Midsummer Festival programme in June 2012. That's when I met Clair McSweeney, the manager of Blackrock Castle, for the first time. She was all business but had this vibrant energy that I really liked. The show went really well and Clair understood what I was trying to explore in the piece. I could tell that she was someone who made things happen, and who thrived on connecting people and on overcoming challenges.

***

I continued to follow people on Twitter who were remotely related to space. I came across Ruth McAvinia, an Irishwoman working at ESA on communications. Her name came up a lot.

I was still terrified of this new 'Astronaut Niamh' life but knew that I had to make this the focus of my next piece of work. I had to explore the notion of activating a dream that had lain dormant inside me for over thirty years, the notion of our place in space and whether we could change it, change our reality.

Then, in 2013, I made an appointment to meet Stephanie O'Neill at Science Foundation Ireland (SFI). She had just taken over the role of managing ESA's Education and Resource Office (ESERO Ireland). I told her that I wanted to do my utmost to get to space, to see what happened when I tried to make the impossible possible. I explained how I wanted to devote the entirety of 2014 to seeing if I could get to space and wanted to create a show around this premise. She liked the idea and advised me to apply for funding through the SFI Discover Programme.

There was only one person I knew who could help me with this – Clair at Blackrock Castle. The deadline for applications was mid-September. A week before the deadline, I plucked up the courage to call her. I told her my idea. She loved it, got it, and instantly invited me to be their artist in residence. We applied for and were awarded SFI funding in early February 2014. As a result I was their artist in residence for an incredible five years.

Having secured funding, I suddenly had another show to create. And a big idea to explore. I researched anyone remotely involved in space and began by sending out a plethora of LinkedIn invitations. It wasn't a particularly successful pursuit, but I did connect with Josh Richards, an Australian communicator, comedian and writer. We hit it off instantly. There were a lot of common interests and a shared passion for space. He was a lot further along his journey than I was, having applied to the Mars One Dutch initiative to send four civilians on a one-way mission to Mars. Josh and I first spoke on St Patrick's Day, chatting for almost three hours. He was very generous with his contacts, and introduced me to senior personnel at ESA, including Juan de Dalmau, who was head of communications at ESA ESTEC (European Space Research and Technology Centre) at the time. In a matter of weeks, I was making genuine connections with people working in the space sector.

And thanks to Blackrock Castle's network of connections and the network of ESERO Ireland, in May 2014 I made my very first visit to ESTEC in Noordwijk in the Netherlands. There I met Juan de Dalmau and Lorraine Conroy, two people who still champion my efforts to get to space. I underestimated, at the time, the importance of that trip. It was a mere three days but pivotal. Lorraine, who worked with Juan in the communications office, chaperoned me over those days. I used the trip to meet Irish people working at ESA. I wanted to know how they had managed to get there, and who had inspired them or shown them a path that I had been blind to.

Lorraine also chaperoned me around ESA's Erasmus Centre, a facility that showcases their participation in human space exploration. They had a to-scale mock-up of the Columbus experiment module (used to conduct all ESA-related experiments on board the International Space Station or ISS), the Mars500 habitat, the Russian Zvezda module of the ISS, the Cupola (a mock-up of the window on the ISS), a lunar rover and a huge wall hanging of the *Earthrise* picture. I had clearance to use all these pieces of equipment to make my new show.

I videoed myself as if I were on the ISS, looking out through the cupola window. I stood in front of that *Earthrise* wall hanging and made it look as if I was standing on the Moon looking at Earth – the very image I'd had in my head since first seeing that picture. The trip had a big impact on me and helped me greatly in writing the show. I was terrified at the prospect of having to write a script about this incredible year, investigating how I was going to get to space. But it was all happening; I was finally walking, in my own way, slowly towards space.

***

To Space premiered in 2014 as part of the Dublin Fringe Festival. It was a very difficult show for me to make because it was so personal. Thankfully, I was surrounded by a fantastic creative team that I trusted. Ronan Phelan and Dan Colley in particular worked with me in devising and creating the show and went above and beyond their roles as director and dramaturge. I owe them a great deal for the commitment they gave me in making it. They gently guided me on how to share key moments of my life.

The show sold out every night.

My parents came to see it. I was terrified of what they would say, given that it's a pretty honest show and quite raw in places. At one point I spoke about Dad's five-year plan, and it was surreal performing it that day, knowing that he was in the audience. He knew the significance of that conversation as much as I did. He was a hero of sorts in that story. I met Dad on the way out of the venue. He hugged me with tears in his eyes, and I whispered a thank you to him. He then started to sob, as did I. I had no words in that moment, nor did he. We both just knew that somehow that conversation had been important in getting me to where I now was. We knew that Dad had done his job as a parent, that he somehow gave me permission to pursue the life I wanted. It still took another few years to do it, of course, but it was the beginning of the change. We are not great with words as a family, but with that reaction I knew that he could see my appreciation for what he had done that day, in his shed, in 2002.

***

Things then started happening really fast. Everything got easier, nothing felt like work, even though I was putting in fifty to sixty hours a week. I couldn't believe the life I was living.

After the Dublin Fringe, we were invited to bring the show to Edinburgh Fringe 2015. And there were requests to perform the show across Ireland too, which we did. Blackrock Castle Observatory were really proud to be involved and found opportunities for me to bring an adapted version of the show to teenagers and school leavers. ESA also seemed delighted with what I had made and were happy to support it by writing about it on their website. Science Foundation Ireland were also very happy with how it went. Karen O'Flaherty, a respected scientist and communicator based at ESA ESTEC, came to see the show, as did Ruth McAvinia, and they both loved it.

It was around this time that Juan de Dalmau suggested that I apply to the Space Studies Program 2015. He also told me about ESA scholarships that were potentially available if I applied by early January 2015. So I did.

In March I was accepted on the 2015 International Space Studies Program, which would take place in Ohio from 7 June to 8 August (a little over nine weeks). Run by the International Space University, this was a residential and professional graduate programme that would attract over 100 people from over thirty countries. I had also been successful in obtaining a partial scholarship from ESA. I paid the €1,000 deposit to accept the place and needed to find the remaining €5,000 fees due before June.

Money was very tight, of course; it always was. But by some miracle I landed a voiceover campaign for SuperValu in April. I would be the voice of their tagline 'Good Food Karma', which would earn me enough to cover the remaining fees. But I still had nothing to cover living expenses. Also, even though it would be full board, I still needed money to cover flights and travel costs. Peter held a charity improv night for me and we managed to raise just enough to cover it all.

In between planning for the nine weeks on the programme, I also had to spend my last few weeks in Ireland re-rehearsing *To Space* for the Edinburgh Fringe run, which started immediately after the programme. In fact, I would have to leave the Space Studies Program a day early to do the technical rehearsal for the one-month run of *To Space* at the Summerhall venue in Edinburgh. It was a very exciting time. I was finally living the life that I'd always wanted.

Still, the last few days before leaving for the Space Studies Program were terrifying. I knew that everything was changing and, as much as I wanted all that was happening, I could already feel the impact it was having on my relationship with Peter. I cried one night with him as I asked what would happen if all these experiences changed me irreversibly or if the life I was currently living would no longer satisfy me. He had had the same thoughts too. We hugged tightly and he told me that I had to live the life that I wanted, and not to be afraid. Whatever was going to happen would have to happen.

I cried some more as he helped me pack my two cramped cases for the trip.

At the airport my bags were over the weight limit and we had to scurry to take things out and re-jig the weight distribution to meet the requirements. We got there in the end and I think that we were both happy with the distraction of it all. When it came time to say goodbye, the moment was excruciating.

One last squeeze goodbye: 'Go live the life you've dreamed of, Niamh. No matter what the cost,' he whispered.

We both suspected, that morning, that nothing would ever be the same again.

Part 2

Activation

I haven't the first clue how to get to space.
So where does one turn when in need of answers?
The Internet of course!

I go online
to the ESA website –
I read that they last recruited in 2009.
The next call will probably be in 2019.
That gives me four years to meet the compulsory
application requirements.

So now I'm online
and I'm checking the criteria.

This is it!
This is what I need.
This is where it begins!

Here we go!

Engineering degree.
I have an engineering degree!

PhD in the sciences.
I have a PhD in the sciences!

An ability to conduct scientific experiment.
Eh, hello? I've a PhD.

20:20 vision.
Hmm, don't have that!
But they accept laser-corrected eyes, so I can do that!

Other requirements, which are desirable, but not essential
are –

A good working knowledge of English.
I'm speaking to you now in English!

Russian.
Spaceba, da, Bolsheviks!

An ability to swim.
Well, I can't put my head underwater but I do a mean
breaststroke!

Oh my God,
I might actually be able to do this!

I can go to space

I can go to space

I can go to space

I can go to space

I can go to space

Space
Space
Space
Space
Space
Space
Space
Space!

– Excerpt from *To Space*, 2014

Chapter 7

Space Studies Program 2015

My flight from Dublin to Columbus Airport arrived in late afternoon on the Friday. We had been told that buses would collect people from the airport the next morning to take us onwards to the Space Studies Program (SSP) at Ohio University in the small town of Athens. As I was too early for that, I stayed in a nearby hotel overnight and got a shuttle bus back to the airport the following morning.

I felt anxious as I headed to the meeting point. It was a moment that I had been dreading. Meeting new people in a big group is my worst nightmare. I get self-conscious. I over-analyse everything I say, what I wear, how I look. But there was another Irish person on the programme, Orla Punch, and we had already been in touch by email and thankfully we arrived at the meeting point within minutes of each other. Norah Patten, an alumnus of the programme, had put us in touch.

And so, together in arms, we joined the rest of the group, a motley but energetic crew of accents and cultures, who all shared a passion for space. From an outsider's perspective you would imagine that the group already knew each other, such was the enthusiasm and banter, but of course we were all meeting for the first time. I realised then that we had all probably felt like outsiders back home. And now, finally, we were all the same. We were somehow normal, or at least felt normal together in this group. It was a nice feeling. I mean, I was still shy, but I at least felt connected to everyone.

There were so many names and countries to remember – Louis from England, Arnau from Spain, Michaela from Slovakia (but her accent seemed English), Reinhard from Austria, Petter from Norway. There were about thirty of us in this group, waiting for the bus to take us to our home for the next nine weeks, where we would be living in dorms together on campus. What had I let myself in for?

The bus finally arrived. Orla and I sat together on the ninety-minute trip from Columbus. I decided to close my eyes. Not because I was tired, but because I had run out of small talk and wanted to avoid saying the type of stupid clichés that you find yourself saying whenever you feel a need to force new friendships. Orla was lovely. She had just completed her degree in architecture at the University of Limerick. Her final-year project had been designing a Mars habitat system, a first for the university, seemingly. She had finished her thesis only a few days earlier (it later won a gold medal, such was the quality of her work). She was easy to talk to, and also understood that sometimes silence was nice too. A few of the others were talking, comparing their CVs or existing connections within the space sector. Some were already working at ESA, some were astrobiologists, engineers, scientists. And some were just like Orla and me, taking our very first steps into the space sector.

Eventually we took an exit off the motorway and the town of Athens came into view. It is a university town, in that there is very little else there other than the university. But the university is very impressive: pristine buildings, leafy parks, playing fields, running tracks. All pretty quiet as we arrived, since most of the students were gone for the summer break. It was nice to see how pretty the campus was and how well kept everything seemed.

It was a relief when we pulled up outside our dorm building, Adams Hall. John Connolly, the programme director, and a crew of people all wearing SSP15 T-shirts, hats and lanyards were standing outside the impressive building, waiting to meet us off the bus. This was John's second year as director and he was on loan from NASA's Johnson Space Center, where he worked on mission planning. John was everything I thought someone from NASA would be. With a subtle Texan drawl, he was warm, affable and naturally commanding in that military sense. While he was friendly, I knew immediately that he wouldn't suffer fools. I sensed that respect was an important value to him.

He shook my hand as I introduced myself. After getting over the usual issue of how to pronounce my name, of course (think of 'Eve' but with an 'N' in front of it, I would go on to say a lot that summer), he said, 'Ah yes! I've already heard great things about you. We're really excited to see what you're going to bring to the programme this summer.'

That seemed encouraging! I took his comments with a smile, though I also felt that the pressure was now on. I needed to bring my best game if I wanted to match his expectations. And that already mattered to me.

As I stood in line to register, I could see that everyone else was at least twenty years younger than me, the average age being probably twenty-two, maybe twenty-three. I decided there and then to commit fully to the summer ahead. As long as I worked hard, I felt that I could prove myself.

***

The SSP is an intense nine-week course. The curriculum covers the principal space-related fields, both non-technical and technical, and ranges from policy and law, business, management and humanities, to life sciences, engineering, physical sciences and space applications. But it is the shared experience of this international, interactive working environment that sets it apart from other educational programmes. Living together in such close proximity, away from other distractions – that is what makes it exceptional. Out of that shared experience, and passion for space, participants create an extensive, international, multidisciplinary network based on friendship and an innate sense of community.

The SSP curriculum includes core lectures covering fundamental concepts across all relevant disciplines (the main thrust of the first three weeks of the programme), while the second phase of the programme (weeks four to six) consists of the 'departmental activities' of the seven SSP departments. The departmental activities include in-depth lectures and workshops, professional visits and individual research projects.

And then the last three weeks are spent focusing exclusively on the 'team projects', in which the SSP participants address a relevant space topic in international, interdisciplinary and intercultural teams. While you will have been working away on the team project from week one, weeks seven to nine are when you exclusively focus on that. Within the nine-week programme, there are other workshops and evening lectures and culture nights, but everything is essentially built around getting you to that team project.

Like I said, it's a residential programme, which means that everyone lives onsite, including the lecturers and staff. Everyone eats together too. It's a key part of the strategy of the programme, isolating us all from family, friends and other external distractions in order to bond as a team and get us over the line in completing that team project. As John Connolly told us on the first night: 'You guys make the programme, getting to know each other, working closely together. And you will learn the most from each other. And form lifelong bonds. SSP is going to change your life.'

I was apprehensive about this forced 'intimacy' aspect to the programme, as I have always enjoyed keeping a professional distance from work colleagues. That was clearly going to be a challenge for me in the SSP environment. The living and eating together part and the evening activities were the aspects that I was dreading most.

There were five of us from Ireland, and I slowly met the others that first day, as people started to arrive. As well as Orla, there was Hugh Byrne, an engineer working at avionics company Curtiss-Wright; Jonathan Faull, an engineer working at UCD; and our youngest teammate, James McCreight from Belfast, who had finished his last final-year exam in aerospace engineering the day before the course started. We were Team Ireland.

In all there were 113 participants from thirty countries and with varied backgrounds; some were already working at their national space agencies, while others were recent graduates from aerospace engineering. And then there were some, like myself, from a non-technology background. But there were very few people who straddled both the worlds of technology and the arts like me. Still, one thing was for sure: while we were a diverse international, interdisciplinary and intercultural group, we all shared one common bond – our passion for space.

***

After one-and-a-half days of orientations and introductions, the programme began in earnest on a Monday night at the official SSP15 opening ceremony, streamed live and watched by Peter and our improv chums back in Dublin. Team Ireland proudly walked beneath the tricolour at the 'Flags of Our Nation' entrance parade with 'Amhrán na bhFiann' bellowing across the auditorium. It was a proud moment, and the first inkling for me that I was going to be part of something truly special.

That night was also the first time that I met a female astronaut, the humble and inspiring Ohio local, NASA astronaut Sunita Williams, more affectionately known as Suni. In her keynote speech during the ceremony, she advised us on how to approach the summer ahead: 'Get to the starting line, be prepared, ask the hard questions, do the right thing. Own up, apologise, admit.' And she concluded with: 'Remember this: you are working for the people on this planet.'

There was a big reception afterwards, where I had time to chat with Suni. It was amazing to have this level of access to an astronaut. I was too shy initially to approach her, but when I saw how amenable she was to speaking to everyone, I swallowed my fear and Orla and I made our approach. She was lovely and genuinely interested in our lives back in Ireland.

Suni is now part of the new corps of astronauts for the US commercial space flights, working with SpaceX and Boeing. In August 2018 she was assigned to the first mission flight CTS-1 to the International Space Station on the Boeing Starliner spacecraft.

I didn't stick around at the reception much longer after that. It was too soon for me to reach out any further to my classmates without that familiar feeling of discomfort arising. So I headed back to my room and got ready for the next morning, our first day of lectures. And that's when the savage schedule really began in earnest.

***

Every morning lectures kicked off at precisely 9 a.m. John Connolly told us that if you arrived on time then you were already late, so this meant getting to the lecture hall for

8.50 a.m. at the latest. There was that military mindset again. He said that it was disrespectful to the lecturer and your classmates to be late. He was right, of course.

The first three weeks were a daily routine of lectures on space law, business and entrepreneurship, policy, satellites, microgravity, orbital mechanics and space. In the first two days, we were also required to select our preferred team projects (there were three to choose from). We got a brief overview of the projects and then we made our selection. I knew that I wanted to be involved in the project titled 'Vision 2040', which was about envisioning the future.

Every aspect of the programme was about space and every lecture was delivered by a specialist in the field; these experts were often flown in from all over the world. And we would get an opportunity to chat with them over dinner, or at the evening lectures or other social events that were part of the schedule. In total, we were provided with over 100 lecturers from the space sector. And so it quickly became normal to live in the company of space architects, engineers, policy makers, or senior management from NASA and CSA (Canadian Space Agency).

Attending social events was also obligatory, as it was all part of getting to know everyone. I really struggled with this. And as expected, I also found lunch and evening dinner difficult. At first, I decided that the easiest way around mealtimes was to sit with the same people at the same table every day, i.e. with Orla and the friends that she had been gathering. Orla was great in those first few weeks and would always include me in her plans, but I soon realised that I needed to jump into this experience head first. So instead I got really good at sitting at different tables, depending on whom I was standing beside in the lunch and dinner queue.

That's how I met Elburz. Elburz Sorkhabi from Canada. He is, without doubt, one of the most unique people I have ever met. I met him about a week and a half into the programme. As people were getting to know that I was an artist of sorts, they would immediately follow up with 'Oh, have you met Elburz yet?' When I finally met Elburz, we hit it off immediately and I genuinely wanted to hang out with him. We became inseparable friends who worked together really well. Elburz is super-smart, with one of the strongest work ethics I have ever known. He is knowledgeable in such a broad spectrum of disciplines and a born leader. Even in the early stages of the programme it was obvious that he would lead our team project, 'Vision 2040'.

But the best thing about Elburz was that he struggled as much as I did with the socialising aspect of the programme. Not for the same reasons, though. He was simply too busy to want to socialise, and always preferred to work rather than hang out. He functioned in much the same way that I did: when in company you give people your energy, but then you need time alone to unwind, re-energise and focus to allow yourself do it all again the next day. He and I skulked away from many social events; it was great. Having a partner-in-crime who was just as interested as I was in working hard, and then sleeping (although he rarely slept, rather just kept working), was brilliant. I'm not sure that I would have survived SSP without him. He kept an eye on me throughout the whole programme and encouraged me to always bring my best game to the table. All this and he was only twenty-five!

There was one bit of socialising Elburz and I could not avoid, however. To help us learn about the diverse cultures of people attending the programme, every Friday night was culture night, where representatives from at least three countries would be selected to do a presentation on their home country. We had been told of this responsibility in the preliminary documentation sent to us long before we arrived. We had been advised about what to pack for culture night and to bring gifts that we could distribute as part of our presentation. So, two days before I left Ireland, I had run into Carrolls on O'Connell Street and bought about fifty tie-pins, each design even more clichéd and tacky than the other – shamrocks, leprechauns, claddaghs, sheep and tricolours. These pins were my contribution to the Irish culture night's booty of goodies.

Team Ireland was part of the first culture night. In preparation, Orla, Hugh, James, Jonathan and I locked ourselves in a room, where we cogitated, deliberated and finally put together our presentation on Ireland, which included a smorgasbord of Irish culture, such as a general overview of the colloquialisms ('What's the craic?', 'James was langers last night', 'That's fierce gas' and other clichés), some top Irish words and phrases (e.g. *An bhfuil cead agam dul go dtí an leithreas?*), making colcannon (a traditional Irish dish of mashed potatoes, often mixed with cabbage), all finishing with a creamy pint of Guinness and a swift Powers for everyone in the audience. It turns out Irish stuff has big value once you leave our lovely island. Those clichés travel well. Who knew?

Really, despite my reluctance to partake in too much social interaction, I was keen to get to know my fellow participants. I just knew that I would have to do it in a way that felt comfortable to me. That's why I proposed hosting workshops in improvisation while I was there. I met Ryan Clement, a writer based in Canada, in the first week of lectures. As we were strolling between buildings one afternoon we both discovered our shared passion for improvisation and decided to work together on hosting a weekly workshop for our fellow participants. About forty people turned up at our first night and it was an instant success. Thereafter, as much as our hectic schedule allowed, we held our improv workshops every week for the duration of the programme. That way, at least, I was getting to know more people.

***

'Splashdown' is a term used to describe the method of landing a spacecraft by parachute in a body of water – it's how the NASA Apollo astronauts returned back to earth at the end of their missions and maybe Orion missions will also splash down in the ocean on their return to Earth in the coming years. Anyway, in advance of the annual SSP Astronaut Panel event, we had a 'splashdown party' to welcome the arrival of the astronauts.

We were graced with space royalty when NASA astronaut

and geologist Harrison 'Jack' Schmitt, from the Apollo 17 mission to the Moon, came to meet and chat with us. Schmitt is the second last person to have stepped on the Moon, whilst also being one of the first scientists there. His mission, alongside Gene Cernan (the last person to leave the Moon) and command module pilot Ron Evans, broke several records, including returning with the largest lunar sample (an estimated 115 kilogrammes). When they returned with that haul of Moon rock, it was distributed by the Nixon administration to the nations of the world, including Ireland.

A quick side note: there's an interesting story to Ireland's Moon rock. A piece of our rock was kept at Dunsink Observatory in Finglas. But after a serious fire in the facility in October 1977, the item was lost. While other segments are also based at the Natural History Museum and UCD's geology department, it is now believed that the missing Moon rock may have been gathered up with all the other debris in the clean-up after the fire. If they had known at the time that the rock had an estimated value of €4 million, perhaps archaeologists could have sifted through the rubble to find it. But sadly that didn't occur. Instead, a piece of Moon rock now lies hidden beneath four decades of rubble at the municipal dump in Finglas.

I was completely starstruck in the presence of Schmitt. I couldn't even speak to him, let alone ask him for a picture. He didn't stick around long and I'm not surprised really. How awkward must it be for him, I wonder, when people look at him with such awe? What question can you possibly pose that hasn't already been asked? For those braver than me who did approach him, he patiently stood and met everyone.

The other astronauts who joined us that evening were Italy's Paolo Nespoli (from ESA), South Korea's Yi So-yeon and CSA's Bob Thirsk. So-yeon was chosen from 38,000 applicants to fly on a sponsored eleven-day mission to the International Space Station by South Korea in 2008. She spoke with us about her eventful and life-threatening re-entry on the Soyuz capsule along with her fellow ISS crew members Peggy Whitson and Yuri Malenchenko. On 19 April 2008, due to a malfunction aboard Soyuz TMA-11, the craft followed a ballistic re-entry that subjected the crew to severe gravitational forces up to ten times the amount experienced on Earth. Ballistic re-entries are very hard on the body and are activated only in cases of severe danger to the crew. Her harrowing story was a reminder to us all of the extreme and hostile environment that space is, as well as the huge risks involved whenever a human leaves this planet.

I particularly connected with Paolo and Bob whilst they were on site at SSP, as they kindly allowed me to interview them. Both of them told me that they didn't really struggle with the microgravity, or the exposure to galactic cosmic rays, or the preparation and planning of EVAs (extra vehicular activities, also known as 'space walks') during their time in space. Their biggest struggle was coping with loneliness and missing their families. They worried for their children, their wives and their parents. The parental instinct to protect and provide was ever-present in their minds while aboard the ISS.

Bob told me that he would take every chance he could to head to the cupola to view Earth. Paolo, a keen photographer who captured some of the best images of the ISS from his first mission on the space shuttle, told me the same. Their perception of and relationship with the planet altered during their mission – they said that initially Earth just looked like a blob of blue, but the longer they observed it, the more they could see: first clouds, then countries. And then cities. Like New York or London or Dublin. And then rivers, and the pyramids of Egypt. And then fires in the Amazon rainforest, the diminishing polar icecaps, and oil spills in our vast oceans.

What Bob said resonated with me and is probably best described by Frank White in his book *The Overview Effect*: 'Earth is a tiny, fragile, ball of life, a living, breathing, moving thing, shielded and nourished by a paper-thin atmosphere. From space, boundaries vanish and the conflicts that divide people become less important. And the need to create a planetary society to protect our "Pale Blue Dot" becomes both obvious and imperative.'[1]

And then there was former NASA astronaut Professor Jeff Hoffman, who lectured us in those first few weeks. He was a terrific lecturer. He spoke to us about his 1993 mission on the Endeavour space shuttle to capture and repair the Hubble Space Telescope. He told us about the radiation in

1   White, Frank, *The Overview Effect: Space Exploration and Human Evolution* (Houghton-Mifflin, Boston, 1987), pp. 3–4.

space, its effects on spacecraft, about microgravity. Someone asked him if he ever worried about the amount of radiation that he had been exposed to during all those missions. He said that he got checked every year at NASA but did remember one night, while aboard the space shuttle during a solar storm, that gamma rays 'pinged' through his brain – he said it was 'like fireworks going off behind my eyes', and then he started to chuckle as he remembered that that night's rest was particularly psychedelic, as the gamma rays continued to shower onto the shuttle, through the spacecraft and 'ping' through his body.

One night the IT team put up a mobile screen and projector and we all watched *Interstellar* on the grass under the stars alongside Jeff Hoffmann. *Interstellar* was a favourite movie for a lot of us at SSP. I looked up to the dark sky above us as Matthew McConaughey's character took off, that great rumbling soundtrack under the action, excellently realised under Chris Nolan's astute direction, helping us all to imagine what it would be like at the moment of launch, the thrust and power, the force on our bodies of travelling at 11 kilometres per second. And I looked to my right. And Jeff was sitting there, just watching the movie, like all the rest of us. And I thought to myself: He's been up there. In space. I'm lying on the grass watching *Interstellar* with one of just over 500 people who have EVER seen Earth from that distance. Now that's something to cherish.

***

Pretty soon, time started to warp on the programme, with very long days of work and more and more activities being squeezed into an already jam-packed schedule. Voluntarily being squeezed in, might I add, as exciting new collaborations began with any number of the multitalented SSP participants. I would be lucky to get, on average, four to five hours' sleep a night. But I thrived on the workload; I was finally being challenged, surrounded as I was by people younger and far more talented than myself. The programme really was unique in that way. I can't remember ever being so motivated around a bunch of people that I'd only just met. And they were people who made me feel that my desire to get to space was an entirely normal aspiration. Maybe my methods of getting to space – as an artist – were different, slightly, but being surrounded by people who remind you that you can do anything if you work hard enough really started to make me feel more confident in allowing myself to want something so utterly impossible.

The pace at weekends was slower and there was more time to work on your own stuff. Elburz and I always had breakfast together at the weekends. Saturday was the day when we took our time over breakfast – well brunch, really (there was no lunch at weekends) – sitting around, finding interesting people to hang out with before we kicked off the team project work, which quickly became the main focus of the weekend activities.

I got to know Roy Naor at one of those breakfasts/ brunches. Roy was also in my team project. He and Elburz had become good pals. Roy had grown up in a kibbutz in Israel.

He was a really chilled-out guy, with big blue eyes; I could tell that he had a big heart and was a real free spirit. But he was also a very smart guy. He was a geologist and was focusing his postgraduate thesis on the geology of Mars. I'd never met someone from Israel before. He explained Hebrew to me and how to make Turkish coffee. He told us that Elburz was the name of a mountain range in Iran and showed me how my name is spelt in both Hebrew and Arabic.

On those long weekend brunches, we could get into an interesting discussion with some of the lecturers on site too. I loved those kinds of chats at SSP, sinking down deep into people, getting to know who they truly were, what they stood for. Those weekend breakfasts were where I had time to properly get to know my new space pals.

By the end of our second week, we had already begun work on our team projects, but the core lectures were still the main thrust of the days' activities. The lectures that week were my favourites. We focused a lot on 'Human Performance in Space', where Dr Erin Tranfield, a space medicine specialist, spoke about the physical effects of microgravity on the human body. We also looked at space architecture. Brent Sherwood, a space architect working at JPL (Jet Propulsion Laboratory, a US centre for robotic exploration for NASA), took us through the design principles for space habitats and the various factors to consider when building homes on extra-terrestrial planets and moons.

Professor Jim Dator from the University of Hawaii was another inspirational lecturer, who lectured us on the societal and cultural aspects of space exploration, governance and forecasting futures. In his eighties, he was a real 'outside the box' thinker, who applauded change and made a big impression on a lot of us. My favourite quote from his lectures was: 'If an idea initially appears ridiculous, then it is worth pursuing.' It was his way of explaining how true innovation or new thinking can initially take time to be accepted by mainstream society. He encouraged us to be brave and bold in our ambitions and was keen to support that approach in our 'Vision 2040' project. He particularly championed the idea of putting artists in space, and understood that our ability to seek out the human aspects of exploration have a vital role in future space strategies. I told him of my aspirations to get to space as an artist and he completely understood what I was trying to do. At that time, when I was just making my first few steps along that path, it was important for me to hear that affirmation from someone as experienced as he was.

Professor Chris Welch, whom I had met back in 2012 at the tweet up at the International Space University, was another lecturer at SSP who understood the merit of artists working in the space sector. Every year at SSP he curated and hosted the 'Arthur C. Clarke Panel' event, inviting creatives who are inspired by space to speak about their work and the importance of the humanities in considering the societal and cultural impacts of space exploration. Thanks to SSP, I began to see that I belonged to a wider network of artists who were inspired by space, and that there were dedicated sessions at academic conferences and meetings where I could meet and learn from this new community. That was so encouraging for me at that point: realising I could meet like-minded individuals who also straddled this science and art interface. Another lecturer, Ginger Kerrick, a pretty senior lady at Mission Control in Johnson Space Center, managed all communications to the International Space Station. She broke it down for us on how it all operated – she told us about the detailed planning and execution of every element of the missions to and from the ISS. At the end of the lecture, Ginger picked up her phone and made a call and then put the caller on loudspeaker – it was NASA astronaut Scott Kelly, who was on a one-year mission at ISS Expedition 43. That's right – we spoke to him LIVE from the lecture hall while he was aboard the ISS.

While that was an exciting moment, my most treasured experience was meeting the humble sons of NASA's legendary Apollo 11 mission, Rick Armstrong and Andy Aldrin. They came in to talk to us about their fathers and about life growing up in the shadow of such influential figures. On 20 July 1969 NASA astronaut Neil Armstrong was the first man to walk on the Moon, heralding a massive first for mankind. He was closely followed by Buzz Aldrin. This moment has had a lasting effect on the world and on our social history.

After being part of such a massive world moment, Armstrong's and Aldrin's lives and the lives of their families were never the same again. Rick told us that his father, Neil, was intensely shy and really struggled with the attention in the aftermath of the Moon landing, whereas Andy's dad, Buzz, relished the fame. They both grew up in the same estate in Houston, surrounded by other families of astronauts; to them, their fathers going to the Moon was normal, everyday. It was only when they moved away from the cocooned community at NASA Houston that they realised the impact their fathers had had on modern society, their contribution to world history, and how many people they had inspired.

But I wanted to know what Neil and Buzz were like as fathers, so I asked the two men what was the best advice their fathers had given them growing up. Both said: 'To do your very best, to work hard, and to respect your neighbours.' It was very moving hearing them say something so simple and honest and humble. Because I realised that no matter whether you landed on the Moon, drove a truck or worked as a salesman, every parent's advice is always the same. And I thought in that moment of my parents back in Dundalk, who had devoted their lives to giving me and my siblings a safe home, sacrificing everything to make us the people we are today. It was the first time since I arrived that I missed home. It seems that no matter where we come from, whatever our culture, we are all essentially the same. Just doing our best.

***

By weeks four and five, I was heavily ensconced in the departmental activities, which in my case were in the space humanities department, co-facilitated by SSP alumni Geoff Steeves (Canada) and Norah, whom I knew already from Ireland. The pace of the programme was beginning to take its toll. Getting a full night's sleep was becoming a luxury and, as a result, a heavy tiredness had started to kick in. I was definitely becoming more emotional about everything. Life was undoubtedly changing for me. I could feel it. One day I would be overwhelmed and frozen in terror, while the next day I would be exhilarated. I wasn't sure if I could return to the way things were before. I'd been exposed to so much already, it seemed ridiculous that I would just go home and continue my life as if nothing had changed. Because everything had changed. For the better. But then I would wonder whether I was brave enough to embrace that change. Change is good, but sacrifice also often comes with change. How do you juggle everything? How do you keep all the great things you already have as you move forward into the unknown?

In the early part of week four we went on the long-anticipated field trip to NASA Glenn in Cleveland, Ohio. Getting to NASA, visiting their facilities, had been a lifelong ambition for many of us. And it was truly incredible. All of it. We saw their largest vacuum chamber (it was huge!), the simulated Lunar Operations Lab, the Extreme Environment rig and wind tunnel, and the rocket propulsion testing facility, each building more impressive than the last.

Seemingly ISU had been negotiating this trip for almost a

year and our great and mighty director, John Connolly, pulled in lots of favours to make it happen. NASA doesn't normally allow non-US citizens to visit their facilities. So we were very privileged to have this opportunity.

The security was so tight, the strictest I've ever experienced. First, SSP staff had to arrange us all alphabetically, and we were assigned a bus to travel on, sharing the journey with colleagues whose surnames were in the same letter range. As we approached the NASA facility, a special security checkpoint had been set up for us. We had to walk off the bus in alphabetical order and check in. When we arrived on site we walked into the facility, again in alphabetical order, and after a passport check we were assigned our name tags and security passes. We couldn't bring in any recording devices or cameras with us and every moment we were there we were escorted by a series of serious-looking NASA security men and their fleet of vehicles. The only photos that we have of the trip were those taken by our designated SSP photographer and the official NASA guy.

The strangest thing about it all was that, in a way, it almost felt like it wasn't happening. Or at least it wasn't happening in the way that I imagined it would. Because I took it all pretty much in my stride. Here we all were at NASA, the place that brought us the Apollo missions and the space shuttle and inspired so many sci-fi films and books, and it felt, well, right. It didn't feel extraordinary to be having such experiences. And I'm not really sure why. Maybe all the weeks at SSP had normalised all the extraordinary things that were happening.

Maybe I was experiencing a version of what NASA refers to as 'Normalisation of Deviance' – a gradual process through which unacceptable practice or standards become acceptable. As the deviant behaviour is repeated without catastrophic results, it becomes the norm. Although, in my case, it would be the extraordinary becoming ordinary. Meeting your space heroes and sharing lunch with space agency professionals had become our norm now. That's not to say that the experience wasn't incredible – believe me, it was. But it just felt that I was ready to visit NASA. I'm not sure if that even makes sense.

I certainly began to appreciate the enormity of the agency that is NASA during the trip – the Glenn research facility is just one of nine centres across the US. Thousands of people are involved in the research and development of each and every part of their missions, every step of each operation being meticulously planned and scheduled. A collective making every element of the mission come together.

We ended the trip with a group photo in front of a launcher and after returning our security passes we got on the bus and headed back to Athens.

***

I think one of the most significant events we had during my whole SSP experience was an evening lecture one night on 'The Human Side of the Columbia Shuttle Accident'. The event focused on this tragic accident that occurred in February 2003 when the space shuttle Columbia disintegrated during atmospheric re-entry, returning from its fifteen-day mission.

All seven crew members were killed in the disaster, the second fatal accident in the space shuttle program after Challenger.

That night we got first-hand accounts of the incident from NASA Johnson's flight surgeon, Dr Doug Hamilton, and our SSP director John. They started by explaining how the accident happened, referring to this notion of 'Normalisation of Deviance' – that's what they determined was the cause of the accident; this had also been the cause of the Challenger disaster. Basically, NASA was doing such a great job in shuttle missions that successful launches became more commonplace, and the enormity of the achievement became less obvious to them. And that is when mistakes can happen.

Normally when you attend these types of event, there's a safe distance between you and the people directly involved in the events being discussed. The facts are analysed, as well as the statistics, and everything is examined from an objective viewpoint. You can observe it all in quite a clinical fashion. No one's really thinking too much about the loss of lives. But it's completely different when two people give their personal accounts of a day when they lost seven friends, detailing the impact it had on them, their NASA colleagues and the families left behind.

Rick Husband.

Michael Anderson.

David Brown.

Kalpana Chawla.

Laurel Clark.

William McCool.

Ilan Ramon.

Seven souls lost.

And while I had read much about this accident, it got a whole lot more real when I was sitting in front of two men visibly moved and still grieving the loss of their dear friends. Both Doug and John worked alongside Laurel's husband, John Clark, a fellow NASA flight surgeon who was part of an official NASA panel that prepared the final 400-page report about the Columbia disaster. But the whole crew were their friends, their work colleagues. They socialised together, they knew each other's spouses, families.

The room was silent and thick with emotion. Unexpressed emotion. What can you say? But we all felt it. To me the silence was more powerful than any words uttered.

As I walked home in silence with some of my SSP colleagues, I realised that I had encountered another aspect of space exploration: our frailty as humans, how truly vulnerable we are, and the massive risks taken each time we launch a human into space. When you hear so much about the successes, you start to believe that travelling to space is safe. It becomes everyday, though of course it's not. I realised that this version of 'Normalisation of Deviance' was an outlook that many of us have when it comes to space exploration. It's only when something goes wrong that we are reminded of the massive dangers involved.

I saw how truly incredible it is to have achieved as much as we already have, and I could also now see the reality of the massive effort of thousands and thousands of people behind every attempt to put a man or woman in space and return them back home safely. And what a miracle it truly is that we haven't lost more astronauts since we began exploring space.

***

We all enjoyed the lectures and departmental activities – they were fun, easy and completely different to anything we had done before. I was particularly proud of the movie that I made as part of the space humanities department team activities, where we worked with the local Athens and SSP15 communities to make a short documentary about 'Dreaming Big'.

But then, as we entered the final phase of the programme, the serious work began. We had been warned for weeks about this final phase: the last three weeks of SSP that were to be devoted exclusively to the team project. This was when the real sleep deprivation would kick in, thanks to the long hours and mountains of work. And the worry about what would happen after SSP ended.

My team project, 'Vision 2040', was about imagining the next twenty-five years – both of the space sector and the wider world – and the steps that we would need to take to plan for a better future. I chose this project because it seemed to suit me best; there seemed most scope for creative thought. Thirty-five other people picked the same topic – including Elburz, thankfully.

The initial stages of the project began in the third week with a Skype call from Gary Martin from NASA Ames. He was our chair (the external manager of this project). Gary is both a scientist and an artist and has a deep respect for others. He was a brilliant chair for our project. He saw his role purely as a facilitator for us to create this project together in whatever direction we felt that we needed to go. We were very lucky in that regard. We were also allocated a team assistant, Aleks, and his role was to figure out the schedule of lectures and visits from the qualified visionaries who came to speak with us and provide guidance on developing the project. We were also assigned our own editor to guide us on the writing process, Ruth McAvinia, who was someone I had already met in Dublin and admired greatly.

One of the main aims of our project was to attempt to predict the space sector in 2040 and specifically how ISU could adapt to meeting the educational needs of such a future. The project criteria were clearly laid out, the objective of the project, the aims, deliverables due, as well as the specific topics that needed to be explored. But how we achieved all this was entirely down to us. No rules; we could run this project in any way we wanted.

In a lot of ways that was the biggest obstacle of all. No matter what expert came to talk to us, or what we tried to do, we could not collectively unlock the mystery of predicting the future in any tangible way. And without agreeing on a coherent vision of the future, we couldn't even attempt to complete the tasks and deliverables that were required.

How do you imagine the future? Where do you even begin to consider what the world will be like in 2040, whether we will have colonised Mars, or mined the Moon and asteroids, or whether we will be living on a massive space station, orbiting our planet? How can thirty-six people agree together on one common future? It was a very difficult thing.

Perhaps our biggest failing was not allowing someone to lead from the first day. There were a few attempts by well-meaning individuals to do that, but it just didn't work. I stood back from this phase of the project, as I found that my voice wasn't heard a lot of the time. Maybe because I was older than everyone else, maybe because I was seen to be an artist in a room of mainly technically minded people, maybe because I didn't socialise with the group in the same way as others did. I don't know. So I took a back seat on all that.

Elburz took a similar stance, although he still applied his organisational skills to facilitate these discussions and adopted a role of collating and collecting the knowledge in the room at each session. He made sure that minutes were kept and that actions and tasks were assigned.

Then time started running out. And the more pragmatic thinkers came to the fore and, finally, after much reluctance – largely thanks to Elburz's ability to corral us – we found our 'roadmap' to the future. It was quite a practical and tangible vision of the future. And it became clear to us that our leader had been in place all along. As Gary, our chair, had hoped, he emerged from the process – as all great leaders do, I think. Elburz was clearly the project leader.

Overall, we were a very happy team who genuinely bonded very well. The other projects had different structures and approaches to getting the job done but never once were any of our deliverables late or rushed. We decided to make our project as visually appealing as the content itself and were blessed with having three talented graphic designers in our team. They created the most beautiful imagery for all our reports, as well as the main image design.

I think that my biggest contribution to the project in those early phases of the planning was bringing the group together as best as I could. We were a group of thirty-six people from a wide range of countries, each with their own cultures and customs. So while someone from Israel might be very comfortable giving honest and direct feedback, our Japanese teammates would never offer feedback unless directly asked, and even then it was difficult for them. Our biggest obstacle was to get buy-in from the whole team, and to ensure that everyone was involved and contributing. Learning how to communicate together was key to that.

In attempting to do this for the team, I enlisted Roy, who shared a lot of my opinions, particularly when it came to everyone having a say in the project. It was clear that fairness and equality were strong values for him. I really admired the way he helped bring the team together.

***

In the midst of completing our team project, I also had a personal project of my own to work on: my presentation of *To Space* as part of Edinburgh Fringe straight after SSP. In the last few weeks of SSP, I had weekly rehearsals via Skype with Sarah, my director. We began with line runs, making sure that I could recall the whole script, and then the later rehearsals were full performances. This was all done so that I didn't land in Edinburgh not having spent time prepping for the month of daily performances, which were due to begin almost immediately after landing.

Sarah suggested that I perform the show at SSP, arguing that I would really benefit from it. She was right, it would be a smart move, and I committed to performing it during the second last week of the programme.

And so the second last Thursday, I performed, without props or technical support, a run through of *To Space* in front of all my SSP colleagues. I had expected a smattering of an audience, as we were all busy by then with our team project duties. However, nearly everyone on the programme came along.

I was terrified; after all, I was the artist and had been saying as much throughout the programme and this was my only opportunity to show them what I did. I made a few mistakes; in fact I lost my way in the script in the first section, though of course they wouldn't have known that. But I got through it.

I took my bow and there was silence. I went to walk away and then they began applauding, stood up – almost the entire room stood up while continuing to applaud – and then there were the hugs, everyone coming up to congratulate me and tell me how much they had loved it.

It was overwhelming and I was so glad that I had taken the risk in sharing my little show with them. I was so relieved afterwards. I hadn't eaten all day, what with my nerves and trying to mentally prepare without distracting myself from the team project too much. Elburz brought me a salad from the canteen for me to eat afterwards, and a bunch of us walked back to our dorms together, all of them so proud of me, hugging and congratulating me again on the show.

It was a lovely night and I felt that support from my SSP community in a way that I hadn't up until that moment. They had finally seen the part of me that I had been withholding. Now that they had seen this other part of me, I relaxed more and I was more myself in those last few days at SSP than at any other time on the programme. And that was a good thing. I only wish I had done it sooner, and been brave enough to be myself throughout the whole process.

***

Given that we had so many technically capable people on our team project, I knew that my best contribution would be to use my creative side and take the lead on our final presentation, an important part of the project. We were encouraged to think outside the box, that a simple PowerPoint presentation wouldn't suffice, and that we should include as many of the team in this presentation as we could.

I thought about how we could present our project in a clear and cohesive way, while also challenging the audience to consider the bigger societal and cultural issues inherent in our project.

Elburz allowed me to run the presentation preparation sessions in any way I wanted, so I began with a think tank, analysing what we thought our project was about. And once we agreed on that together, we brainstormed ideas on how best to represent that, whether it was a movie or an image or a dance or a piece of music.

Everyone went away then and started creating, buzzed up and motivated to try something new. Oriol and Saho, two of my colleagues who were fast becoming good friends, created a game to demonstrate potential new forms of online education. Oriol was from Barcelona and had become smitten by Saho from Japan pretty much the first day that they met. They were a devoted pair, doing everything together, including writing the code for this game. Another pal, Roy, made a short movie, while Michaela wrote an inspirational TED-type talk, and our youngest participant, Niti from India, wrote a beautiful and heartfelt poem. And then it was our job to find a way of threading these activities together throughout the presentation.

I was interested in my participants' views on the future in relation to their families. I wanted to know what their concerns were for the future. I emailed all the participants and asked if they would pose that question to their families. I got a load of different responses, many of them concerned about the availability of valuable resources, the threat of war, poverty, education and inequality.

I was also interested in the rich diversity of cultures and languages and skills that surrounded me that summer and that had such a positive impact on changing any unconscious bias I may have had in terms of race, age or ethnicity. I wanted elements of those ideas to be a part of our final presentation, as they were themes that we constantly returned to throughout the whole programme, not just our team project.

Most of the content was coming together nicely. The work ethic and commitment in delivering this work was astounding from the whole team. But we were all very tired by this stage too. Juggling a tight deadline with giving constructive feedback proved difficult on occasion. Most people, when they asked for feedback, listened and could see the merit in making a few tweaks. But there was someone whom I offended terribly when he came looking for feedback and that was my dear friend Roy.

He had spent days working on a short movie that reviewed the legacy of the Space Studies Program, using both existing and new footage to tell the story. He was exhausted, having dedicated hours to learning how to use the editing software on his computer, as well as creating his movie. But when he showed it to me I could see that it could do with a bit of a clean-up edit-wise – nothing major, just some small tweaks – and I felt it would then look magnificent. Being tired myself, my manner in delivering that feedback was off that afternoon and I really upset him. We had an exchange of words –

nothing offensive, Roy would never offend – but damage had been done to our friendship. And it killed me.

I knew that it was my responsibility to fix it. I wasn't getting much sleep by then anyway but had even less that night, trying to figure out how best to make amends with my lovely Israeli pal.

I went straight to our workspace the following morning, knowing that he tended to arrive early. I sat beside him as he was editing the same movie that had caused the argument, and quietly apologised and told him that my friendship with him meant more than any stupid movie. So we talked it out and thankfully by the end of this extraordinarily awkward but loving conversation we got through it. And my awful feelings of guilt and shame around how I had behaved lifted. He was quiet that morning but later in the afternoon he came back to me with some of the edits completed. He had done a wonderful job and once he handed it over his mood also lifted and we were back on track.

I know that the argument may seem trivial, but it was a moment when I saw an ugly side to myself and I didn't like how I had behaved, how I had communicated with someone who was a lot gentler than I was. I've never forgotten it and when Roy and I worked together again, it was something that was ever-present in my mind.

Finally, after gathering together everything that people had made, I saw that we could nest these creative pieces together between sections of the final presentation. I related the idea back to the team and, after a few adjustments, this became the skeletal structure of the final presentation. Lastly, we agreed on how to divide up the technical content of the project into different sections, assigning two people to present each section. We had our final presentation structure.

It was going to be quite a tricky sequence of activities to manage, so I took the role of stage manager and we rehearsed together every detail so that nothing would go wrong on the day. We had to keep to a strict one-hour time limit and would be docked a point for every minute that we went under time or over time. Thanks to the keen eye of those engineers, we pared down every segment of the presentation so that collectively we had the whole thing running at exactly an hour.

The last few days of the team project were tough on all of us as deadline after deadline had to be met. First we had to submit the executive summary, which took up a big chunk of the graphic design and the editing teams' time. Once that was done we had about another two days to get the final report submitted on time, again putting huge pressure on the writing and editing teams. And then everyone came together to deliver the final presentation.

Elburz was liaising between all the teams and managing everyone; I really don't know how he did it. We weren't getting to hang out as much and, since he was my closest friend at the programme, I was spending a lot of time in isolation, which was not really ideal. So we came up with an idea to watch movies together on Saturday nights, take the odd late walk and then head back to work. That kept me going; he probably never knew the importance of those interactions for me and I was truly blessed to have him there. He was my pal, everyone's pal. So it was no surprise when the participants voted him to be our class speaker, meaning he would make the final address on behalf of us all at the graduation ceremony.

***

Soon it was the morning of the presentation and it was my turn to take the reins and make sure that I delivered for the team. I got to the theatre ahead of everyone else and checked and double-checked all the technical equipment, as I didn't want anyone getting spooked by a technical hiccup. I created a space for props; I walked everyone through where they could find everything that they needed. I supported any of the speakers who had last-minute nerves. And then we began.

I kept a watchful eye on everything, assisting the team in any way that I could from the stage wings, trying to make them as comfortable as possible. I held my breath, watching the clock to check that we were going to finish on the hour exactly as we had planned. And we did it. We got to the last piece of the presentation, where everyone gathered on the stage as Niti recited her poem. And we were done. Everyone did a great job.

Once it was finished, I slipped away and had a bit of a cry to myself. I was proud of the work that I had done. Proud that everyone was so happy with how the presentation had gone. Proud that I had overcome some of my biggest challenges in getting all the creative elements to come together as a cohesive whole in the presentation.

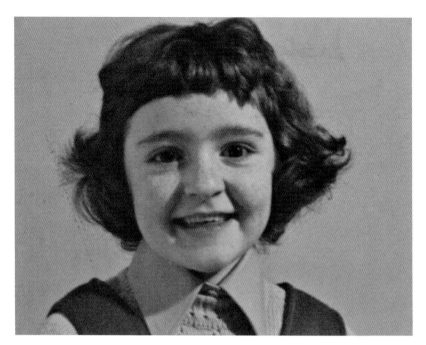

Me at about ten or eleven years old, taken at Scoil Mhuire National Girls School in Lucan, Co. Dublin *circa* 1980. (*Author's collection*)

On holiday in Co. Kerry in July 1981. *Left to right:* Dad, Mam, me, John and Deirdre. Tom is in front of John. (*Author's collection*)

A still from the 2015 production of *To Space* at Summerhall during the Edinburgh Fringe Festival 2015. (*Courtesy of Conor Burnell*)

Promotional picture for the first run of *To Space*, taken at Dublin Airport one quiet Sunday evening. (*Courtesy of Naoise Culhane*)

Speaking at InspireFest at the Bord Gais Energy Theatre about the big space dream in July 2017. (*Courtesy of InspireFest*)

Field trip to NASA Glenn as part of the International Space University's annual Space Studies Program 2015.
(*Courtesy of the International Space University*)

The Ilyushin plane where I got to experience the sensation of weightlessness. I remember being really nervous when this photo was taken and wondering what I had gotten myself into. (*Courtesy of Space Affairs*)

In mid-flight during the Zero G phase of the parabolic flight in August 2017. This image is taken from the footage I obtained from my GoPro. (*Author's collection*)

You can just about see me at the very back of this photo. This session of freefall is quite near the end because there are fewer of us in the picture (the others are recovering from illness at the top of the plane), and also because I'm not holding on to the bar. (*Courtesy of Space Affairs*)

My Zero G travelling companions, taken at the gates of Star City just before we headed off to the airfield. *Left to right:* Tim, Mazdak, Matthias, Claudia, Susi, Nikola (Die Astronautin candidate), Lena (our translator), Mannfred (standing behind Lena), me, Galina, Insa (Die Astronautin candidate), Rok and Norbert. (*Author's collection*)

Crew 173 and some of Crew 174 stand side by side outside the Mars Desert Research Station, Utah, to officially acknowledge the end of our mission and the beginning of that of the Planeteers from India. (*Author's collection*)

A group photo of my crew mates, taken on our very last EVA, just hours before the arrival of Crew 174. Waving the flags of our home countries during EVAs became a thing in our photos as our mission progressed (I'm not sure why). Roy is lying on the ground, Idriss is sitting on the rock and Rick, me and Michaela are standing. (*Author's collection*)

Rick, our GreenHab officer, hard at work on Sol 5 in the GreenHab. This was where he spent most of his time during our mission.
(*Author's collection*)

When Roy returned home, he worked with colleagues and SSP alumni from his country to establish their own analogue Mars facility, DMARS, at the Ramon Crater in the Negev desert. They had their first mission in February 2018 and Roy invited me to attend. This picture was taken by Crew DMARS-01 while on EVA. (*Courtesy of DMARS-01 crew*)

The Soyuz MS-09 rocket arriving at Launchpad 1 (aka Gagarin's Start) on Monday 6 June 2018. It would take Alexander Gerst (ESA), Serena Auñón-Chancellor (NASA) and Sergey Prokopyev (Roscosmos) to the International Space Station two days later. (*Courtesy of Space Affairs*)

Launch of Soyuz MS-09 on 8 June 2018. (*Courtesy of Space Affairs*)

So our SSP experience was effectively done; we just had to wait to hear our final scores for our team project (we were to receive a score for each element of the process). Gary asked us all to return to our workspace as he shared our final score with the room. We did very well, with the adjudicators saying that it was one of the best presentations they had ever seen.

The team project was never really about envisioning the next twenty-five years (well, yes, to a degree it was), it was really about finding new ways of working together in a diverse cultural mix of language, work practices and disciplines. And different mindsets. It was about bringing together big thinkers, objective engineers, scientists and artists in a room, who all had very different ways of seeing the same thing, and leaving them to figure out a common language. Keeping everyone together, moving forward together.

And therein lay the true experience of SSP15. But you only learn that by going through the process. I learned so much about myself and how to communicate in a multicultural and interdisciplinary working environment in our team project.

I also learned a whole new level of work ethic and commitment. I was fortunate to spend nine weeks with some exceptionally gifted people who shared my passion for space, but who also were some of the hardest workers I have ever seen. The commitment and quality of work from everyone was extraordinary. And something that I had never seen before. It made me see how anything is possible if I am surrounded by people at the top of their game, motivated by a common passion. That's how stuff gets done!

We all headed together as a team to a local bar to celebrate our success. This would be my last night with everyone, as I had to pack my bags for the early morning flight that would bring me back to my old life in Ireland. I was going to miss the graduation ceremony in order to get to Edinburgh in time for my run of *To Space* at the fringe festival.

As part of the graduation ceremony, the SSP director, John Connolly, places a special International Space University pin on your lapel to officially mark you as an alumnus of the programme. I was sad at the prospect of missing this; however, knowing that I was set to leave early, John came to the bar where we were all celebrating and did a sort of impromptu graduation ceremony for me, officially placing my pin on my team project T-shirt. It was a lovely moment and typical of John, who had considered every detail of the programme from start to finish. I thanked him for all his support and told him that he had been right when he said on the first evening of our SSP experience that it would change our lives.

***

I needed to return to my room to begin packing. I had accrued a ton of space-related books and stickers and pins, as well as extra clothes to cope with the hot Ohio summer. It was going to take me a while to get through it all. Everyone else headed onwards to more bars in Athens. I promised that I'd join them once I'd packed, but I didn't.

Elburz had also returned to his room, so instead we went for one last walk together around midnight. There wasn't much to say; we had been at SSP to do a job and the job was done. I thanked him for taking care of me and we promised to keep in touch. We had already made plans to work on a couple of STEAM engagement projects with Oriol and Saho. I was determined to keep him in my life, as I felt that he was a wise soul who had already shown me not only better ways of working, but also better ways of leading and communicating. He was a real friend. I was going to miss our daily routine of working together and being in the company of someone who had a great calming effect on me. We hugged it out, promised to keep in touch, and I went back to my room to have a little cry to myself. I knew that I was going to miss Elburz terribly.

I got up the next morning and headed off pretty much straight away. Orla messaged me to make sure that she saw me before I left. So, as I emerged from the lift with my bags, she was there, already in tears and finding it difficult to say goodbye. My first friend at SSP was one of the last people to say goodbye to me.

As I left the building, I heard a huge roar of 'Wait!' It was Oriol. He had heard that I was leaving and scrambled down from his room to see me. He gave me the tightest squeeze, full of sincerity. No words were exchanged. There was no need. It was a very moving moment; I hadn't realised how much our friendship had meant to him. I left in tears, waved at them and then I was gone. Heading back to Ireland.

We can often underestimate how close we can get to people in a short time and, consequently, how strange it is when we're no longer around them. I had spent up to sixteen hours a day with these people, ate almost 200 meals with them, and had rarely been apart from many of them for the sixty-three days that we spent together on this programme. I would really miss them.

I grabbed segments of the closing ceremony from the live stream on my phone while on the move but didn't get to see Elburz's speech until much later that night. I was missing everyone, especially my core people – Elburz, Oriol, Saho. We had already begun to message each other within an hour of my leaving Ohio. And it was reassuring. I knew that the friendships that I had made at SSP were genuine.

But then I had no time to even think or process everything that had happened during the summer, because the second I landed in Dublin I had to completely switch focus. Edinburgh required my immediate attention.

Chapter 8

The Deorbit and Cost of Dreaming Big

It's hard to describe the festival season in Edinburgh; you need to experience it for yourself. There can be up to 3,000 shows on every day. It's impossible to keep on top of everything that's happening – there are so many venues, so many people, so many terrific shows on in every available empty space in the city. If you were to go to ten shows a day for the full duration of the festival, you would still catch only about twenty-five per cent of the official programme of the fringe festival. The pace is hectic. Everywhere you look there are show posters (just when I thought I had seen them all, I realised that I just hadn't walked far enough). The streets are packed with tourists, festival goers, street performers, musicians, magicians, and 'flyerers' gently coaxing you to come to their show. It's exhausting just to walk the Royal Mile, let alone join the flyerers to promote your own show, but thankfully I had a great support team in my producer, Joanna, and technical crew, Conor and Liadain (who were also ace flyerers). Sarah, our director, came along too for the first week of the run, as did Peter. He has great skills in promotion, having run a comedy club at The Bankers Bar for over ten years. It was nice to have him around, but there wasn't much time to reconnect properly, since we were sharing a rented house with so many other people.

And so the daily schedule went from being all about space to all about *To Space*. And making sure we had an audience. Which, thankfully, we did. Being a part of a curated programme of science-related shows at the Summerhall venue beside The Meadows was a big bonus. But that still didn't stop Joanna and Liadain getting into their spacesuits every day to hand out flyers on the crazy Royal Mile, while I kept the box office and its environs stocked up with our publicity material. Because, in Edinburgh, you can take nothing for granted. No amount of reviews or media coverage will guarantee a full house. It's a hard graft and an expensive month for all involved. So much so that to have a run at Edinburgh where you break even is considered a success. (None of it would have been possible without the support we received from Culture Ireland, and I was so proud to have been provided with that support.)

Overall, the run was a success. We broke even, we got positive reviews, and there was a natural interest in my personal story about getting to space. I was fortunate to get some great media coverage, as well as interest from other festivals asking me to bring the show to their 2016 programme. For example, we were invited to bring the show to Australia's big arts festival, Adelaide Fringe, as well as to the Edinburgh International Science Festival and to other venues across the UK.

***

When I got back home to Dublin, I began taking stock of the previous few months and the world that had been opened up to me. We had been warned that readjusting to real life after SSP would be difficult for many of us. They called it the 'deorbit'.

And my deorbit after returning from Edinburgh was a struggle. I had just been exposed to the world that I had always wanted to be a part of; as a result, I found that my drive to step further into that world was all-consuming. I spent hours working on the computer, tirelessly driven to reach the next step of the journey.

Peter suffered the most from it all, I think. I knew that our relationship was different after my return; it was difficult to get back to where we had been before. The change had already started the year before, really, ever since the moment I had realised what I wanted to do with my life. Since then, it was as if nothing else mattered. All our common interests in comedy and performance were no longer there, with our improv comedy club closing the year before and the shift in my career away from full-time performance and towards this middle ground between science and art. He did his best to support me, but something fundamental had changed. I knew it and he knew it. Still, I wanted to keep everything, of course, and was determined to at least try to incorporate this new life into the old one.

I was still in constant contact by WhatsApp and Google Chat with people from SSP, trying to keep abreast of what everyone was doing, keen to remain involved. This was especially true when it came to the purported plans for a simulated Mars mission.

In November 2015 Arnau, an SSP15 alumni pal, got in touch to tell me that he was leading a submission to the Mars Society for the simulated Mars mission that had been spoken about so much at SSP. The group was making an application to the Mars Desert Research Station based in the Utah desert in the US for early 2017. He asked if I would like to include an art experiment as part of the application. At this stage, all six slots to participate in the actual mission were filled, but I was next on the list if someone pulled out.

I took a look at the Mars Desert Research Station online, and remembered that Michaela, one of my 'Vision 2040' teammates, had spoken about her experiences there while at SSP. So I assisted them in developing a communications and outreach strategy in their submission. This step of the application process didn't take long as it was simply an initial request, but if this was approved we would be required to complete a more detailed experimental protocol before being allowed to continue to the next stage.

Arnau got back to me a few weeks later to confirm that we had progressed to the next stage of the application process and I would now need to provide a more detailed plan for the next round. And by early 2016 one of the original six crew, Parker, had pulled out, which meant that I was now officially a crew member for our potential mission. My chances of experiencing a simulated Mars mission were increasing. The deadline for submission of my experimental protocol (which was the communications and outreach strategy) was St Patrick's Day 2016. This was also the day that I would return from Australia after touring *To Space* at Adelaide Fringe.

Peter and I worked together on planning the logistics of the tour to Australia. There was a lot to organise. We brought Sarah, our director, and Liadain as technical operator, as well as the two of us to present *To Space* to Holden Street Theatre for a one-week run. Peter became our production manager and did an awesome job of sourcing from Dublin the various elements of the set that we would need when in Adelaide; he also arranged travel for Sarah, Liadain and the two of us, our accommodation, publicity and everything we needed to prepare in advance of the run. I'm not sure if he really enjoyed the job, but we figured that if he produced the show then we could make a sort-of holiday of the tour. He did it for me, I now know.

It was going to be an expensive tour, largely covered by Culture Ireland funding, although I still had a little money coming in from the SuperValu voiceover campaign. Additionally, I had been invited to speak at a panel event in Brisbane as part of the World Science Festival, which was to take place about a week after our run at Adelaide. So I agreed to do it and we planned a holiday travelling up the east coast for Peter and me after the show's run. I hoped that maybe we could rekindle our connection if we got to spend quality time away together.

The show went really well at Adelaide Fringe, receiving four-star and five-star reviews. And more requests to return it for a longer Australian and Asian tour, if we wanted. Peter and I flew to Sydney after the run and hired a car to allow us spend a week travelling slowly up to Brisbane for the World Science Festival gig. It was a lovely holiday, overall, although we were sometimes not on the same page.

We got back to Dublin on the evening of 16 March. After a twenty-three-hour journey, I was pretty exhausted. But I got up the following morning and spent the whole of St Patrick's Day completing the arts/outreach strategy and experimental protocol for our application to the Mars Desert Research Station. I had promised to make the deadline so I stuck at it until it was done and then went straight back to bed after I'd uploaded the files to the shared Google folder. Afterwards, I pretty much put it out of my head; there was a lot more to think about at that time – other funding submissions, keeping money coming in with role-play and communications workshops, etc. My stash of savings had gone on the Australia trip and it was time to knuckle down.

***

Soon I managed to wangle a visit to ESA's Astronaut Centre (EAC) in Cologne as part of my research for what would be my next theatre show. It was my first trip of many to the facility and Dr Aidan Cowley, who works at the centre, proved to be a great host/chaperone during that trip. I was given an extensive tour of the centre, and saw the facilities used to train astronauts from ESA, Roscosmos, NASA, CSA and JAXA for their missions to the International Space Station, including the neutral buoyancy facility – a 22-metre-deep pool used for EVA (extra vehicular activity) training for astronauts. Aidan arranged for me to meet with Jules Grandsire, head of communications at EAC, and told him about my theatre project. He offered his support.

With this level of ESA support, I was confident that my application to the upcoming Science Foundation Ireland Discover Programme round of funding to create the show in partnership with my buddies at Blackrock Castle Observatory would be successful. I spent a pretty grim June bank holiday weekend in 2016 getting this application – as well as one other – over the line. I think that I sat in front of the computer for fourteen hours straight, focusing entirely on the screen.

That same month Arnau officially invited me to Crew 173. I would be joining Roy, Michaela, Idriss and Arnau from SSP15 and an SSP14 alumnus named John. Our application had been accepted and our mission at the Mars Desert Research Station (MDRS), the one-hundred-and-seventy-third mission (hence the Crew 173 moniker), was scheduled for early January 2017. I was happy, but immediately started fretting about how I was going to finance the trip. The fees were hefty for non-students – to attend the MDRS I was going to have to find $2,000 (postgraduate students fees were less at $600). On top of that, there were flights and travel costs to consider. But I think if you really want to do something, you always find a way.

Thankfully, I didn't have to pay the entire fees straight away – fifty per cent was required as a deposit and the remaining fifty per cent was due six weeks before the mission began (so, in late November 2016). I found the money to pay for my flights to Denver, but I still needed to finance my travel from Denver to Grand Junction, where I would meet the crew and begin our journey together into MDRS. All in, I would need about €4,500 to cover everything.

A part of me thought that by the time the mission came up, I would probably be unable to do it, that my place would be given to another person. But as the months went by, I was somehow still a part of Crew 173. We officially accepted our offer from MDRS that summer, I found the $1,000 deposit and hoped that I'd find the money for the remaining costs by November.

The crew communicated regularly – mostly through WhatsApp calls – in the months leading up to the mission. At the last minute the crew member named John, who I hadn't yet met, pulled out and Richard Blake came forward to accept the slot. He was Australian and also an alumnus of SSP, though from the year before the rest of us. I wanted to know everyone as much as I could before we were living together in confined quarters for over two weeks in an extreme living environment, so, for me, those WhatsApp calls were as much about getting to know everyone well as about the logistics of the mission.

This was all very exciting, but like I already said, there is often a cost when extraordinary change comes about in your life. And the biggest cost to my life so far has been the loss of Peter. As the months passed, it became clear that we could no longer get back to the way things once were between us. We often argued about my lack of work–life balance. But I didn't care about balance, I had finally found my passion in life and I couldn't let anyone take it away from me. As I set off on all my new space adventures, I was leaving him behind and there was nothing more that we could do about that. He wanted me to be happy and although I did want to be a good partner to him, it was clear that I wasn't succeeding and something needed to change.

I returned to the Space Studies Program in 2016 by invitation from the co-chairs of the space humanities department – Norah and Geoff from my SSP15 summer. I was to run communications workshops as part of their schedule of activities. That year, it was hosted at Haifa in Israel and was John Connolly's last year as director.

It was so great to see some of my SSP15 alumni again – Petter, Michaela, and so many more. While the trip was just a week away this time, it was enough for me to realise how happy I was to be back among my space community. On my last night there, I was sitting on the beach with my colleagues, talking about the SSP experience. Soon we were discussing the detrimental impact that the programme had on people's personal lives, listing off a bunch of people who, after completing the programme, had ended their long-term relationships, as they knew that their lives had changed irrevocably. I sat in silence, listening to the discussion, because I knew exactly what they were talking about. I had tried for a year to deny the change in me, as well as my desire to want more from life, but now it was time to do the right thing.

I flew back the next morning. Peter was there to collect me at the airport. It was quiet between us as we drove into the city. I headed to bed pretty soon after getting back home. I got up the next morning to find him making me my favourite breakfast of pancakes. I couldn't take a bite. Instead I said that I had to tell him something. In moments, we were both crying.

He hugged me tightly and whispered, 'Just say it, Niamh. I know what you're going to say, so let's do this.'

So I did. I told him that I needed to be on my own, how I couldn't give up on my dream and that our relationship had to end. He knew it too; had known it for months. While it was an awful day for us both, it was also a relief. We had come to the end of our thirteen years together in a calm and respectful way. We had given it everything and it was time for us both to part ways and get on with living the lives that we both wanted. It was the right decision, as painful as it was. I owe him a great deal; he has been a big part of my life.

***

In September 2016 I met up with three of my soon-to-be analogue astronaut crew at the International Astronautical Congress in Guadalajara, Mexico (where Elon Musk famously unveiled his grand plans to colonise Mars). Arnau, Michaela, Idriss and I discussed fundraising efforts to cover the costs of our Mars mission. Michaela had secured her travel and experimental costs, as had Roy. Arnau, Idriss and Richard, as students, had much lower fees to pay than I did. I had the most money to raise, all without the connections that most of the other crew members had obtained. At this point, it wasn't looking likely that I was going to secure the deficit from anywhere other than my own pocket.

I was attending the conference in Mexico to present a paper about *To Space* at the 'Arts and Space' session. My session was chaired by a Mexican artist, Nahum. We had met briefly in Haifa while he was attending SSP16, where he shared some of the exquisite work he had created while on a zero gravity flight in Moscow some years previously. It struck a chord with me, and I realised that I wanted to one day explore zero gravity for myself, to see how I would cope in those circumstances.

The congress was huge. I loved once again being a part of this community and reconnecting with space pals from the arts and sciences. I left the congress charged with new ideas and inspirations and delighted to feel part of an ever-growing network of collaborators and colleagues.

***

I returned home to a silent house. Peter had moved out while I was away. As sad as it was that our relationship was over, I felt happier. I knew that I needed to focus exclusively on my work. My dream to get to space was growing with every new adventure and project I undertook. I had to give it one hundred per cent if I was to have any chance of success.

My 2017 was going to be a busy one, after all, beginning with the simulated mission to Mars.

Part 3

Mars

MANNED MISSION TO MARS
Mars.
The Red Planet.
Our nearest neighbour.
And fourth planet from the Sun.

Some scientists believe, or have the theory that,
in the past Mars may have once been a thriving planet
very similar to Earth.
That water may have flowed across the surface in rivers
and streams,
and that vast oceans covered the planet.
That Mars was once an oxygen-rich atmosphere.
That Mars may have been like Earth once.

Another theory held by some scientists believes that life on
Earth
may have originated on Mars,
that tiny bacteria-like life forms were transported here
via meteorites,
which means that we may essentially be Martians.

Theories are great.
But we don't know anything until we test the hypotheses.
Until we go there for ourselves.
To Mars.
A human mission to Mars.

NASA and the European Space Agency are in full prepa-
ration mode for their mission.
On the Orion Spacecraft, due for launch in 2036.

But the pressure's on.

They're not the only ones.

Private enterprises like Mars One,
a non-profit organisation based in the Netherlands,
intends
to establish a permanent human colony on Mars by 2027.

The NASA-led Mars mission
and Mars One,
these missions couldn't be more different.

For space agencies like NASA, ESA,
their priority is the safe return of their crew.
Getting them home is as important as getting them there.
And that's why it's not happening until 2036.
They're waiting until they can bring their astronauts back.

Whereas for Mars One, the prime objective is to establish
a new permanent colony on Mars.
They believe this to be an opportunity for civilians to be
pioneers of human space exploration.
To begin life again on another planet.
In return, they will have to die on that planet too.
Because once they land, they'll never leave.

But there is always a cost.

Do you stay and wait until it's the right time?
Or do you take a leap of faith and hope for the best?

Where do you even begin in trying to make the impossible
possible?

– Excerpt from *To Space*, 2014

Chapter 9

Mission to Mars

Mars is hot right now (not literally: it's actually very cold). SpaceX launched a car to the planet as part of their Falcon Heavy rocket launch in early 2018 and NASA's Curiosity Rover, which landed on Mars in 2012, has been sending us images of its arid surface for some years now. If we are to believe media reports, our travelling to Mars seems tantalisingly close. But is it? Are we really as ready as they say? We might be able to deploy rovers and cars to Mars, but humans are a whole other matter. How do we prepare astronauts psychologically and physically for living in isolation for sustained periods of time with limited water, food and power? How will they cope on lengthy journeys across the vastness of space to reach our nearest planetary neighbour? Where do you start? As interest mounts in Mars, many countries are looking to analogue missions as a possible platform for providing such answers.

Since 2001, test facilities simulating conditions on Mars, known as analogues, have been in existence in desert, volcanic, polar and underwater aquatic environments in Hawaii, Chile, Canada, Spain, Florida and both polar regions. Each analogue specialises in specific aspects of living in the extremes, whether it be human factors (such as psychosocial and/or scientific studies of crews), procedures, or testing prototypes of specialised equipment (such as rover or spacesuit designs). Logistical and scientific protocols for missions are always tested and re-tested before launch. And this becomes all the more critical if those missions are human missions. Analogues are an important element of their success – and this includes the facility I would be staying in: the Mars Desert Research Station in Utah.

The MDRS is equipped with a permanent habitat, science dome and observatory. Situated on the San Rafael Swell of southern Utah and located 11.63 kilometres by road north-west of Hanksville, the desert's Mars-like terrain can simulate working conditions for scientists and engineers on the red planet. The facility has already hosted 194 crews (as of August 2019) who experienced realistic EVAs (extra vehicular activities) in spacesuits under simulated conditions. Beyond the scientific studies at MDRS, the station is also a useful platform for human operations training.

The main purpose of my involvement in heading to Mars was to spread the message of space to the general public. Very few people know or understand much about the research already occurring across the globe. I felt that, with my experience in communicating science, I might be able to do something to remedy that. I knew that I could make use of this mission to Mars, and share my experiences of living in extreme conditions with a team of people that I barely knew when I returned to Ireland. Speaking of which, it's probably time that I tell you a little bit about my crew mates, Crew 173. I've already mentioned their names, but here's a little more about them:

Roy Naor, Geologist and Crew Health & Safety

I first met Roy at the Space Studies Program. We were working on the same team project together. He seemed like an old soul to me and we bonded over his Turkish coffee. He was completing a Masters degree in geology, specialising in the geology of Mars. Roy speaks with a smile and the first thing he told us when he introduced himself was that he had just proposed to his girlfriend at the airport with a violin, not a ring. Roy always sees the best in people; he's a peacemaker and a worrier. Roy has become a bit of a celebrity in Israel because of this mission; it turned out that everyone in his country knew about him and our mission.

Richard Blake, Astrobiologist and Crew GreenHab Officer

I first met Richard, or Rick as we called him, in Grand Junction, the first morning we arrived. Rick was completing his Masters degree at the University of New South Wales in astrobiology. He's a monster of a man, broad and tall, reaching somewhere near 6 foot 4 inches, I think. My first impression of him was that he was shy and quiet, and very laid back. We had spoken together a few times on WhatsApp as we planned our mission but that was it.

Idriss Sisaïd, Engineer and Crew Engineer

Idriss is originally from Morocco, his father from the Berber settlements in the Atlas Mountains. But now he is based between Paris and Nice. He studied engineering in the top university in France and became an entrepreneur who had designed a solar-powered generator. He wanted to bring a prototype of his 'OSol' generator invention to MDRS as part of his experimental mission, but the paperwork became too difficult in getting it through US customs.

He's a funny guy and a talented actor too. I discovered all this when we spent time together performing improv comedy while at the Space Studies Program. He claims that our preparations for the Crew 173 mission saved his life. On the evening of Bastille Day in 2016, we delayed his plans for getting to the festivities happening in Nice's town centre as we had scheduled a WhatsApp call for that evening. When our call ended, he headed towards the town centre to meet up with his colleagues, only to find everyone fleeing in the opposite direction. That was the evening of the terrorist attack on Nice, when a white van drove into the crowd along the promenade.

Michaela Musilova, Astrobiologist and Crew Commander
Michaela is from Slovakia and is well respected in her field of astrobiology. She's tenacious and very thorough in all her affairs. While we were both attending the Space Studies Program our paths rarely crossed, even though we worked together on the same team project. She seemed nice, though, with a wicked laugh and a great sense of humour. A respected and well-known scientist in her home country, her involvement in this mission was extensively covered by Slovakian national TV and press in the weeks before it began.

Arnau Pons Lorente, Engineer who never arrived at MDRS

Arnau is from Barcelona and he and I had worked together a lot while attending the Space Studies Program, especially on the team project. Arnau was originally supposed to be commander of our mission, but two months before we were due to begin, his schedule altered and he had new commitments to his PhD at Purdue University. So we planned that he would join us just a few days into our second week at MDRS. As a consequence, it made sense that Michaela be commander of the mission. But the more I travelled towards Hanksville, seeing how remote it actually was, the more I began to realise deep down that it was unlikely Arnau would ever make it to MDRS. Sadly, after all the work he completed on our application, he never got to be part of the mission.

***

I was very apprehensive about the mission. I really didn't have a clue what I was getting myself into. Apart from Roy, I hadn't really spent time with any of the crew while at SSP. Michaela, Roy and Rick were experienced scientists and geologists in the field, i.e. they were used to being outdoors, collecting samples in extreme environments. Roy and Idriss were already great friends, and had spent a lot of their time at SSP together. I was also a lot older than any of them. But I kept my concerns to myself.

I wanted to impress them, prove that I was a valuable crew member. As head of communications, I took responsibility for promoting the event and leading efforts in a crowd-funding scheme for the mission. I wrote a short script that I got each of them to record, and out of this I compiled a promotional video for fundraising as well as publicity purposes. It was good, but while it helped with raising awareness online about the trip, it didn't help significantly with getting money in to cover everyone's expenses.

Still, despite my funding issues, there was undoubted interest in my simulated mission. I spoke about my trip on radio and at private events, and some schools asked me to talk to their students about it. I was invited by Science Foundation Ireland to speak with Dara Ó Briain about my upcoming mission at their Science Week 2016 flagship event, 'Scintillating Science', held at the Mansion House, Dublin in mid-November. The producer interviewed me in advance of the event and asked me to stress the scientific merit of the mission, as opposed to the artistic and human components. While it's vital to have a scientific aspect to the mission, to me the most interesting part of being a member of Crew 173 was going to be the human aspect of the experience – how five people got along living in a confined space, in an extreme environment, shut off from friends and families. I wanted to capture that aspect of the experience most of all, by sharing how I coped. That way, I could include everyone in the mission, science and non-science audiences alike.

By November 2016 the money I needed to cover the trip hadn't come in. I decided not to approach Culture Ireland for corporate sponsorship or any financial support; I didn't think that I should. Being without that financial support, or sponsorship, certainly gave my mission an added layer of complexity and pressure. In the end, I managed to scrape enough money together to cover costs, but it was very tight.

My family thought I was mad, heading off to the desert to live with five other people I hardly knew. Over the Christmas break, I shared our promotional video with Mam and Dad. I could see as they were watching it that they had concerns. They asked me some questions, but my answers didn't seem to change their opinion. In fairness, they didn't try to dissuade me. I think that they simply didn't understand what I was trying to achieve in completing a mission like this. And they were probably also worried for my safety.

Overall, it was a strange Christmas in 2016, very low key, as I knew that I would be in the middle of the Utah desert a little over two weeks later. It was also my first Christmas on my own in thirteen years. I wanted to celebrate that I was finally putting my personal quest firmly ahead of everything else. I got up Christmas morning and went for a long walk in the park. There was no one about; I liked it. I liked the solitude; in fact, I had really started to need solitude. It felt as if I'd always been in a relationship or thinking about some- one; this was the first real time in my life that I was genuinely on my own. For the first time in a very long time, my own company was more than enough. I was enough. Space had given me that self-belief back.

I think that's been a big part of it for me. Once I rediscovered this passion for space, everything in my life immediately got better. My mind was calm. I had lots to celebrate that Christmas Day. I had come a long way, and was about to embark on the next chapter in my adventure.

Chapter 10

Crew 173 Mission

The Mission: Crew 173 Simulated Mars Mission 14–29 January 2017.

Facts about the Mission: The mission will take place in the Utah high desert in January at the Mars Desert Research Station (MDRS) through the Mars Society.

Mission Objectives:

1. To 3D print a modular brick and investigate proof of concept using these bricks for building future homes on Mars.

2. To conduct a number of astrobiological experiments using soil and crops.

3. To complete a number of outreach activities during our time at MDRS. (This was my main mission goal as crew artist and I spent my days with GoPros, a 360 camera, and my DSLR camera and voice recorder, capturing content to share on social media with our followers.)

   The overall aim of this outreach project is to capture the public's interest in Mars, MDRS and space:

   • by telling the real-time human story of our mission pre-, during and post-mission

- to inspire the younger generation to pursue STEAM education and realise that everyone can play a part in the exploration of space

- to raise awareness of the importance of analogue missions, specifically MDRS, and the opportunity for non-space agency individuals to play their part in human space exploration.

***

My contribution to the mission began in earnest about a month before we were due to meet. I had assigned homework to all the crew to make short one-minute videos of their preparations for the analogue mission: speaking with their families, answering specific questions that were assigned to each of them about their preparations, hearing the thoughts of their families and loved ones, stating what they believed would be their greatest challenge on the mission. I also asked them to share their travels as they headed towards Grand Junction, where we would all meet on the morning of Saturday 14 January 2017.

In early December we were sent the 'Crew Packing List' document by the programme manager for MDRS. This was the opening paragraph:

These lists are suggested equipment for each MDRS crew member. They do not cover all details of what you should consider bringing for your rotation.

Environment
The MDRS is located in the high desert plateau country near

Hanksville, Utah. Weather can range from pleasant to very hot or cold, depending on the season. In winter and early spring, temperatures may drop well below freezing (20°F or approx. -5°C, especially early in the morning) and rise to very pleasant levels (60°F/15°C on some afternoons). The air is usually very dry, but it may snow, sleet or rain. Winds can peak to 50 kts and wind chill is an important factor to consider. The area can be muddy during the rainy season (October through March). Late spring and summer are usually quite hot and dry (100°F/ 37°C daily highs), and afternoon thunderstorms are common in the highlands. Flash floods are a potential hazard. If you plan to do fieldwork, familiarise yourself with basic desert safety.

Basic desert safety? That short paragraph suddenly made it all very real and scared the bejesus out of me! The recommended packing list that followed was extensive too, with over fifty items listed, some of which were specific to field study work – items like rock hammers, hand lenses, waterproof field study books and pens, i.e. probably standard items for geologists and all those who regularly work in the field. But there were also a lot of practical items that I simply didn't have, including a decent pair of hiking boots, a sleeping bag, a headlamp, stocking cap, thermals and waterproofs.

I followed that packing list to the letter, as I didn't want to die in the desert and wasn't going to take any chances. I spent a lot of time sourcing everything recommended and spent a small fortune too, spending hours online or in Great Outdoors and other camping shops. I also knew that I needed to upgrade some of my camera gear, though it was an added expense that I hadn't really foreseen. But at least I knew that all this equipment would be useful for future activities. And indeed it has been. These items were an investment in me, and in my commitment towards my big dream. And so, as people were running around Dublin doing their last-minute shopping the week before Christmas, I was buying thermal wear, hiking boots and socks, camera protection hoods, gloves, sunglasses and waterproofs. I borrowed whatever I could, like saloupettes (trousers typically designed to be worn during snowsports) from my sister, and the headlamp from a friend who fishes.

I had hoped to travel light, but with all the technical equipment, basic clothing items and everything else on that packing list it was proving difficult to squeeze it all into my luggage while keeping within the airline's weight restrictions. Thankfully, I managed to get everything into one suitcase, but only after three attempts. In the end, I took two pairs of trousers, a pair of saloupettes, four thermal tops and underwear, a single sheet, a quick-dry towel, a sleeping bag and small pillow, hiking boots, scarves and gloves, a computer, my Canon Eos camera and two lenses, a GoPro and new 360 camera (although I never got good footage from it), a 2TB external drive, batteries, a charger, a notebook, a first aid kit, some pictures that my brother Tom's two children had drawn for me, and vitamins. And my Lottie doll.

In early December, I had been approached by The Lottie Doll Company, based in Donegal, asking if I would like to bring their 'Stargazer Lottie' with me on my mission. Lottie dolls celebrate childhood and promote the empowerment of children by encouraging kids to be themselves, to play imaginatively and adventurously, and to have fun. The values behind the Lottie doll were similar to my own. And as well as that, 'Stargazer Lottie' had already flown in space, on board the International Space Station in 2016 as part of ESA and UK astronaut Tim Peake's mission. I knew immediately that this was a great idea, and an opportunity for me to connect with young girls, so my new Lottie doll got packed into the case.

***

I didn't sleep a wink the night prior to my flight. I was up late packing, rearranging everything so I could fit it all in. I had a shower, then checked and rechecked my travel documents. I was too excited and anxious about what lay ahead. I wondered what I had agreed to and whether I was going to cope in this new world of extreme environments and with living in such close proximity to others.

The alarm went off at 3 a.m., but I was already awake. The time had arrived and, after all the months of planning and preparation, I was finally heading off. I made my final pre-mission video in the apartment, capturing my last gulp of coffee, me locking up the apartment, the last moments before pulling out the door at about 4.30 a.m. to head to the airport.

It was a dry and very cold morning, but since I was wearing so many layers of clothes (to save some space in the case) and schlepping an awkward and heavy case, I was already sweating. Back in 2003, 11 January was supposed to be the day that I emigrated to New Zealand to begin a new life in Nelson. I reflected on this. What would have happened had I taken that job? I couldn't imagine that I would ever have found my space career if I had taken that path.

***

My journey to Grand Junction, where I would meet the crew, took over two days. I arrived in Denver on the afternoon of the twelfth (I took a cheap flight with a long layover at Amsterdam), and the next morning took an eight-hour Greyhound bus to Grand Junction, Colorado.

The bus journey was pretty scary. It was ultimately destined for Las Vegas and so had attracted a party crowd. Other than one backpacker, the passengers were American and all pretty wild. A lot of them appeared to be drunk or high on some substance. There was lots of banter, but with a dark, aggressive tone between the mainly male passengers. I was beginning to regret my decision to 'see America by bus' instead of via the Denver–Grand Junction flight, even if this option had been a lot cheaper than flying.

In the first few minutes of the journey, there was an

altercation between the driver and a guy who seemed drunk. As the driver was reading out the rules by which all the passengers were required to abide, this guy was talking and making jokes about the rules. So the driver pulled over and ordered him off the bus. I was sitting at the front and didn't dare to look back towards the drunk passenger, but I could hear it all kicking off a few rows behind me when the driver went down to speak to him. I assumed this bus ride would be like all the others I had ever taken, like the Mathews bus home to Dundalk, or the Aircoach to the airport. A quiet and subdued experience, where everyone more or less kept to themselves. This was an entirely different thing, with a whole load of tension – guns were even mentioned.

People continued to scream at the driver, while others were screaming at the drunk man to calm down. Across from me was a woman who looked as scared as I felt. She smiled nervously at me; we were both in this together. Finally, the drunk guy was escorted off the bus and things calmed down. The driver had won, so the mouthy passengers knew that they had to rein in their wild behaviour. But I didn't feel safe for the whole journey.

We stopped a couple of times along the way. I kept my head down and enjoyed the stunning winter views on that 350-mile journey across Colorado. I reached Grand Junction about 7.30 p.m. that evening. Idriss and Rick were already there but were too tired to meet up until the morning. Michaela and Roy were stuck in Denver Airport. Their flight to Grand Junction had been cancelled due to the weather.

Michaela and I had been due to share a room in the Days Inn hotel, which was a pretty dingy place, though they had a special discount rate for analogue astronauts heading onwards to the Mars Desert Research Station. But since Michaela was stuck at the airport that night, I had a room to myself. These would be my last few hours of solitude before meeting up with everyone in the morning. In hindsight, I was glad that I'd taken the bus and not flown from Denver.

The Days Inn really was a miserable place. The bed was bumpy, the sheets were off-white, the walls had that brown cigarette-stained hue, as did the curtains and netting on the windows. But the room rate was reasonable. It was freezing that night, around minus two degrees Celsius outside and so I had to switch on the heater – a loud and large rusty contraption attached to the wall that blasted out hot air. In no time I was gasping for water and had to switch it off, but then it got cold again, so I realised that I would have to leave it on all night. I didn't sleep much. The cause probably wasn't so much all the appliances bellowing all night, it likely had more to do with the apprehension I felt for my imminent adventure with a bunch of strangers. I was completely out of my comfort zone.

To clarify, I love the outdoors, but I'm not an experienced outdoors person. I wasn't even in the Girl Guides growing up. Apart from my days of camping across Australia on my gap year, I didn't know much about surviving in extreme environments, miles away from civilisation, let alone how to simulate living on another planet. My only preparation for what lay ahead had been getting everything on the list that we were given by the MDRS director, and asking Michaela a gazillion questions.

I also had a huge task ahead of me: recording practically every moment of our shared experience at the Mars Desert Research Station, as well as managing our media to the outside world on a very slow broadband connection. Did I have enough memory cards? Did I have the right camera lens? Would I be able to complete my own personal art project while there? (I still didn't know what it would be as I needed to spend time at MDRS to figure that out.) I was also anxious about living with people I really didn't know, who were all twenty years younger than me, from different countries, high achievers and used to getting what they wanted. How was I going to get on? In the end, I decided that my best strategy for the next two weeks would be to just go with the flow, relinquish the fear, trust in the moment and embrace the experience. And that's exactly what I did.

***

On Saturday 14 January, I met up for the first time with my full crew. I met Idriss and Rick at 7 a.m. for breakfast at the Days Inn. In our first few hours together, I babbled a lot and was overly enthusiastic about everything – even at 7 a.m. That's me when I'm nervous – filling the silence. I was worried that Rick might be moody, but he seemed to know a lot about the landscape and, while he was often quiet, when he spoke he had something interesting to say.

As we waited for Michaela and Roy to join us, the three of us picked up from the airport the two four-wheel-drive vehicles that had been assigned to us by the MDRS director. Soon we were driving around the sprawling metropolis that is Grand Junction (that's a joke, Grand Junction is probably the size of Dundalk), running some small errands in convoy.

I used the time to get to know Rick better. He seemed like a pretty laid-back guy and the more time I spent with him, the more I knew that we were going to get along fine. Idriss was on the hunt for build materials (aka filament) for the 3D printer, an essential piece of equipment for one of our key experiments. Shannon Rupert, the director of MDRS, had confirmed that there was a 3D printer at MDRS that we could avail of, but Idriss estimated that we would need to source more filament to complete our building design. Since it was a Saturday morning, all the companies we visited in Grand Junction were closed, so we just had to hope that a previous crew had left behind a big enough stockpile of filament.

Finally, around 12 p.m., Michaela and Roy's flight landed. We picked them up at the airport and drove back to the hotel to load up our luggage. I was relieved to see that, apart from Rick, they'd all brought luggage just as huge as mine.

I travelled with Rick and Roy as we drove the two-and-a-half-hour trip to Hanksville, the next stop on the journey to MDRS and the last town before going off-road. Idriss and Michaela travelled together in the other vehicle.

Roy and Rick were discussing the geology of the landscape as we began to approach the arid Utah desert. Roy had extensively studied the topographic maps of the region in preparation for the mission, and was very familiar with the parts of the landscape that we would explore while at MDRS. He was a mine of information on all the geological points of interest along the ride, pointing out Triassic rock formations and explaining how these formations occurred. It was a whole new world that I knew little or nothing about.

I couldn't get enough of these stories, sitting forward so that my head was between Rick and Roy, looking out in fascination at the bizarre landscape around us, with its lack of people, towns, flora or fauna. I was happy in the knowledge that I was going to be hanging out with people who could teach me a lot and who were involved in some very interesting activities.

Chapter 11

Landing on Mars

We arrived at Hanksville around 2.30 p.m., already over two hours late for our meet-up with Crew 172. Hanksville was hardly a town. In fact, it was more of an ordinary stretch of country road where you happened upon a cluster of a dozen or so houses located around a junction. No street lights, one set of traffic lights, no signs. There was nothing for miles around, just this one road, where at a small junction there was a petrol station and 'Brenda's Diner', while a few yards down the road there was a small restaurant, another smaller petrol station and a small white grocery store with no name on the front. Everything was dusty, rusty and dingy.

We were looking for 'Bull Mountain Market' and turned around in the jeep, thinking that we must have missed it. This was where we were supposed to meet Crew 172, who were taking us to MDRS. We drove back to the petrol station at the junction, where Michaela enquired about the location of Bull Mountain Market. The owner informed her that it was the tiny white shop at the other end of the road. So we headed back there. But there was no sign of Crew 172. Likely because we were over two hours late, due to Michaela and Roy's delayed flight.

The store seemed to have many functions: as well as being

a regular grocery store, it had a whole back section stocked with the kind of food needed for living in the extremes – freeze-dried egg, potato, butter, etc. The kind of food that we would have to eat while at MDRS. Our supplies were also stored there, ready for us to pick up. We took a look through the boxes; it was pretty basic stuff, all dried goods. So we decided to pitch in about $20 each to buy a few extra food items to tide us over the first few days (or Sols, should I say). We got some vegetables and fruit, which probably wouldn't last long, of course, but we'd make them stretch for as long as we could. Those items were also to go towards our 'culture night' dinners – a throwback to SSP. I threw a bag of potatoes into the basket, since I'd be making shepherd's pie for my 'Ireland Culture Night'. We packed our food into the two jeeps. It was a tight fit, what with our huge luggage already squeezed into the back.

Bull Mountain was also a kind of pizza takeaway/ restaurant and a clothes shop of sorts. We decided to eat pizza and drink brewed coffee as we waited for Crew 172. As commander, Michaela called Shannon, the MDRS director who managed the facility, to see if she had any update, but her phone rang out. However, soon after that, she received an email from Shannon with a cell number for Patrick from Crew 172. Michaela called the number and Patrick explained that they had headed back to MDRS after waiting for us. He promised to return to pick us up soon. So we waited. An hour went by, still without a sign of Crew 172. Michaela called again and I ordered more pizza and coffee.

At 4.30 p.m. Patrick and Anushree, members of Crew 172, arrived. I noticed how scraggy they both appeared – they were filthy, especially their boots and trousers. They looked exhausted and gaunt, but both were welcoming and friendly and keen to help us in any way that they could. They took a look at our two packed vehicles and we considered the logistics of fitting us all into their MDRS vehicle, along with all our food and gear. We had been instructed by Shannon to leave the hired vehicles at Bull Mountain, and we would all travel in on the one MDRS jeep, a dilapidated, smelly and rusty thing desperately in need of a valet clean. But instead Patrick wisely suggested that we drive one of the hired vehicles in, behind the MDRS jeep. That way we could bring everything in one trip. It also meant that Crew 172 could leave MDRS in the morning in the hired jeep, and we wouldn't need to drive them to Bull Mountain in the MDRS jeep. Shannon didn't approve of crews doing this, as the valet bill for the hired vehicle is hefty after driving across the harsh and muddy MDRS terrain. But it was getting late, and we knew that when we finally arrived at MDRS there would still be a lot of procedures training for us to complete before darkness fell.

As we moved our bags and groceries into the MDRS vehicle, I became embarrassed that Patrick and Anushree could see all our food and stuff. They asked us what we'd bought; they seemed especially interested in the food. I felt territorial of our provisions, realising for the first time that our diet and choice of food was likely going to deteriorate during this mission. Poor Patrick and Anushree probably hadn't enjoyed a tasty meal in a long time.

I felt another wave of anxiety. What had I gotten myself into? Still, I followed Roy and Rick into the MDRS vehicle, squeezing myself in. I wanted to stay near them for now; they both made me feel safer. Idriss and Michaela drove their vehicle behind the MDRS vehicle, now accompanied by Anushree.

Hanksville disappeared quickly behind us. We drove for ten minutes, then Patrick took a right turn onto a dirt road which soon devolved into a sort of track. We soon found ourselves slowly negotiating our way between huge boulders and rocks. No wonder the MDRS vehicle looked so wrecked; this was very harsh terrain to manoeuvre for any vehicle. We travelled very slowly, keeping an eye on Idriss driving the hired vehicle behind us. He was doing brilliantly; I'm not sure if I would have had the courage to drive on those treacherous paths.

Patrick shared stories about their mission experience, especially all the times that things went wrong – how they didn't have water for two days because the pipes froze. He repeatedly told us to protect our pipes from freezing during our mission. We got it. We won't let our pipes freeze! Listening to him, it felt as if he was weary from it all. His role in the crew was as their GreenHab officer, which was the role Rick would have in our crew. This meant that they both had responsibility to maintain and grow any vegetables or plants in the green habitat (which is effectively a greenhouse, and is commonly referred to as GreenHab). They engaged in an extensive conversation about the GreenHab, which had just recently had a rebuild. A fire had occurred in the GreenHab the previous year, as someone left the gas heater on overnight to keep it warm for the plants. But something caught fire in there overnight and the unit went up in flames. Crew 172 had been the first crew to avail of the newly refurbished facility. I don't think that Patrick got to plant much during his mission – the cold weather didn't help. Instead, he spent a lot of time setting up the new GreenHab, building shelves and organising all the new equipment. On the plus side, everything would now be in great shape for Rick to begin planting.

There was a lull in the conversation and Patrick asked us again about what food we had been allocated. I was glad that Roy and Rick were with me; in a matter of hours, it felt that we were somehow already Crew 173, feeling separate to Crew 172.

As the drive continued, Patrick gave us good advice on how to drive through the harsh landscape. More horror stories of their mission were shared. We listened, trying to absorb it all, but it was too much information. Without really understanding just how extreme MDRS was, it was difficult to appreciate the advice that he was so generously sharing with us. But I certainly had never experienced terrain like it before; it seemed ridiculous to try to even drive over some stretches. The boulders were huge. My head had banged off the roof of the vehicle far too many times already; the shock absorbers must have worn out long ago.

Finally, after what seemed like an eternity, the track levelled off and a sort of dirt road appeared. It led us into a series of shallow valleys, winding between small rocky hills. Then we turned one last corner out of the hills and there it was: the Mars Desert Research Station. We had arrived. My home for the next fifteen days. I took in the view in front of me: the round tall building, the main habitat (often referred to as Hab), the GreenHab, a dome building (called the science dome) and the observatory. I was finally here.

But just because we were on site didn't mean that our mission had begun. We wouldn't start until Crew 172 departed the following morning. And until then, we were not yet on Mars; we were just guests of Crew 172. In limbo, somewhere between Earth and Mars.

The MDRS vehicle pulled up beside the Hab and we all piled out. The light was fading and it had already started to get cold. I looked around the facility; everything looked pretty worn and broken. Patrick had gone into the Hab. We all did that thing of stretching unnecessarily and yawning and pretending to be interested in the smallest things, because we didn't know what we were supposed to do. Nobody was telling us what to do. It felt as if we should wait to be invited into the Hab, rather than walk straight in of our own accord. I mean, they may have wanted to tidy it up before we entered, or they may have arranged something special for us, or they might want privacy in their last few hours at MDRS. It was, after all, still the home of Crew 172. We didn't know whether to unpack the vehicles or wait. After a few minutes hanging around outside, Patrick re-emerged from the Hab and invited us to bring our food and gear in.

***

When entering the Hab, you leave your shoes in the airlock. This is vital and the only way to keep dust and dirt to a minimum. I mean, it is pretty filthy anyway, but keeping muddy boots outside makes things a little cleaner. This meant that we were all required to wear slippers once inside. The Hab is a steel building with lots of sharp edges throughout the structure, so these slippers were our only protection from all sorts of hazards.

The Hab has two storeys. The ground floor is an engineering area used for maintenance activities, as well as to suit up and run experiments. The toilet, sink and shower are also on the ground floor. Upstairs are the living quarters. Every crew member gets their own quarters, or 'state room'. But until Crew 172 left, we had no quarters of our own. So we had to leave all our luggage and food on the ground floor of the Hab, and it occupied most of the free space on the ground. This made me feel even more uncomfortable and in the way. As a result, I clung to Roy and Rick for company.

Slowly the rest of Crew 172 – minus their commander

– emerged to greet us. As we mingled with Crew 172, we were told again about the freezing pipe, and that Patrick was making dinner for us all. They all seemed to possess that same unhinged energy, as if they were on edge or excited or something.

Ilaria Cinelli, their commander, appeared about forty minutes after our arrival on site. She instructed us that we needed to take the official two-crew handover picture straight away as the light was fading fast outside. For this, each crew wore their official flight suits, displaying their crew patches. Crew 172 dispersed in all directions to acquire their flight suits. Michaela had our flight suits in her luggage, and she had to trawl through all her gear on the ground in the Hab to source them. She had had them made by a seamstress colleague of hers back in Slovakia, which had saved us a lot of money.

As she distributed our flights suits, we all took a good look at them, as it was the first time we had seen them. Ours were navy and the mission patch that Idriss had designed for us was emblazoned on the top right pocket. Mine was quite big on me, but that was no harm. It meant that I could wear lots of layers underneath. But Rick's flight suit was a very snug fit and was clearly catching him around the crotch area. Michaela, never having met Rick before, was unaware just how tall and broad he was. He ripped the inner leg pretty much immediately and I noticed his embarrassment, so I made a joke to disperse the tension. The flight suits were great; they certainly looked the part. And even though the material was thin and flimsy and nowhere near the quality and durability of the official ESA flight suit that I had worn back in 2011, it didn't matter, as we would use them only in these rare official photo ops and when we went out on our EVAs.

Crew 172 reappeared, some returning from outside, some from the living quarters upstairs. Their flight suits were a bright orange, in sharp contrast to ours. Ilaria corralled us all to stand on the steps outside the Hab, with us on the right-hand side and Crew 172 standing on the left. Our commanders stood in front. A timer was set on their camera, we heard the click and the official picture was done.

Immediately after, Ilaria instructed her crew to begin our training and thus began an extensive tour of the facility as the crew shared procedures with us on how best to suit up, how to use the radios, how to do daily checks and daily reports, how to communicate with mission control and so much more. There was way too much information thrown at us. One of the crew, Troy, was particularly keen to explain everything to us, so much so that after the training ended, he continued for another hour with Idriss, our crew engineer. Anushree showed us around the science dome, Patrick led us through the GreenHab, and we also got a brief 'health and safety' tour. But I had stopped listening by that point; there was too much information to take in. I hoped that there was a manual somewhere that I could study on my own afterwards.

**

The living quarters on the upper floor of the Hab felt instantly different to the rest of the facility. They felt strangely familiar, and warmer, and the lighting was a lot better too. It was the heart of the facility and immediately made me feel calm. We were all upstairs together by this stage and all feeling a lot more relaxed.

Patrick was making dinner for us as we struggled to find somewhere to sit. It was a bit of a squeeze, though, with twelve of us in a facility designed for six/seven people. As we waited for dinner, we all paired off with those with our equivalent roles, so I chatted extensively with Nick about his role as crew journalist for Crew 172. He had just submitted his last report. He shared some good tips on filing all the photos and videos that would accrue each day, or should I say 'Sol'. He found the role to be quite high-pressured, having to make sure that the daily creative report was ready for 7 p.m. every day, along with at least five photos, summarising the crew's activities. He explained how each photo had to be reduced in size to about 100KB to upload effectively. This would also need to be done for any videos that I wanted to submit. Submitting the daily reports is an important part of the role of crew journalist. We have a two-hour window every evening to communicate with CAPCOM (our mission support, who communicate with the crew from 7–9 p.m. via email), to submit our reports and for them to instruct us on what we need to focus on for the next Sol.

As we began to settle into our new environment, I noticed how Crew 172 repeatedly asked Ilaria for their phones. She replied that everyone would have their phones once all the daily reports had been uploaded to CAPCOM. This reminded her to tell us that the broadband was very limited and she had to confiscate phones to ensure that they had sufficient data remaining each day to submit the daily reports.

Upon hearing that the reports had been submitted, Ilaria then went to her state room, returning with a basket of phones. The crew retreated feverishly once back in possession of their phones, each going online, checking their texts, emails, Facebook. It was an unusual, almost-feral moment, a glimpse of who I might become by the end of our mission. It sent a shiver down my spine.

Once dinner was ready we were handed a plate covered in tinfoil. We had already been advised to adopt this practice for meals, as it saved water for washing up. Ilaria and Anushree were particularly attached to this notion. Rick, who I had already figured out was someone who championed sustainable living, questioned them about the wastage of tinfoil to offset this water conservation. They didn't reply. I didn't question the practice and took the tinfoil-covered plate graciously. But I have to admit that after a few mouthfuls, it was certainly weird eating food from a bowl covered in tinfoil. Plus, I had managed to puncture the tinfoil covering my plate. Now what? I asked them what they did when it happened to them, as I'm sure that it must have. They advised that because of such situations it is handiest for everyone to keep track of their own cup and bowl and to take responsibility for the cleanliness of their own utensils. I nodded cordially.

After dinner, the crew opened a bottle of sparkling apple juice to share with us, wishing us a successful mission. It was a lovely gesture and we shared this moment together – an end to their mission and a beginning to ours.

Not long after, a lady appeared at the top of those dodgy steps suddenly and roared: 'Well hey! Do we have a party going on?'

It was Shannon Rupert, the programme director for MDRS, who lived on site to manage the station and operations. She lived in a trailer just over the hill and stopped by each time a new crew arrived. We had been expecting her, as she had to take us through the regulations of MDRS and we had documents to sign. If we were in need of anything, she would be there for us. She seemed nice, but tough. She stayed for about an hour and we made a plan to meet her the next morning to train us on the ATVs (all-terrain petrol-driven vehicles) and Moon buggy vehicles (electrically charged), weather permitting. Shannon had already been living at MDRS for about two years. She hadn't been on site during Michaela's previous mission at MDRS, however.

Everyone headed off to their quarters pretty soon after dinner and the five of us were finally left alone in the dining area, each inflating a temporary bed for the night. There was so much that I wanted to talk to them about, such as their first impressions of everything. But I thought better of it and decided to keep my thoughts to myself. It was only about 9 p.m. and a lot earlier than I had imagined the crew would go to bed on their last night together. I got the feeling that retiring to their rooms was more to do with a desire for privacy than tiredness. We had all run out of polite conversation.

As we all prepared for bed, regular trips up and down the steps were made, as well as trips to the toilet. Every time someone flushed or turned on the taps in the bathroom, I noticed the honking sound of the water motor kicking in, a loud and regular goose-like honk that disturbed every one of us in the Hab. Eventually everyone settled down for the night.

I couldn't sleep. It didn't help that the bed was deflating slowly beneath me as I lay there. Nick and Patrick were downstairs and I decided to join them for a chat. They were both so giddy and excited that I wasn't quite sure how to take them. They told me that I would understand when I got to the end of our mission. I asked them if it had been difficult and they both nodded. They were both glad to have taken part in the mission, but they couldn't wait to get back to the real world. They intimated how difficult it was to live in such confined quarters, cut off from everyday life, and how easily tensions could build. Patrick and Nick talked about the food they wanted to eat upon their return to Earth, how drunk they were going to get, how they couldn't wait to have ice cream, chips, beer. I was slowly beginning to appreciate how the confinement had affected them. As much as I didn't want to return to the floor upstairs, I imagined that they probably wanted to spend their last few hours together and were probably being very well-mannered in tolerating my company. So I thanked them for their time, said my goodbyes and returned to my inflatable bed.

***

I must have nodded off at some stage, because I awoke with feet and legs walking around me on the floor. Crew 172 were up and starting to pack and pull out. I pretended to be asleep; I was too tired to make polite conversation any more and, at this stage, I just wanted them gone.

I wanted our mission to begin with my lovely Crew 173. I found it strange that I already felt so close to them; maybe it was because this experience was so beyond my comfort zone and I needed to rely on them. I wasn't sure.

About thirty minutes later, Ilaria climbed the stairs and called out her goodbyes. We thanked her again and wished her goodbye as she warned us that the toilet had blocked and that we would need to figure that out first thing. We all slowly rose from our inflatable beds and watched Crew 172 drive away in the jeep; we were still wearing our sleeping bags. And then they were gone.

The atmosphere instantly felt different. It felt like Christmas morning. We were finally alone and had the Hab to ourselves. In minutes, we had each selected our 'state room' and were unpacking groceries, gear, clothes. Perhaps there was already a hint of that same feral behaviour I'd noticed in Crew 172. But what of it?

We were now officially on Mars.

Chapter 12

Begin Transmission

It had rained quite heavily overnight, so the terrain outside was very muddy and we were confined to indoor duties for our first Sol. After unpacking food supplies and selecting our state rooms, we had our first breakfast of oatmeal, Cheerios and dried apple, washed down with an assortment of tea, coffee and, for some, nutritious servings of Tang.

Our first group decision was establishing the parameters of living at MDRS and determining the limitation of our simulation (SIM) experiment. It's an important factor to consider. For instance, in the past, some crews were known to break SIM on Sundays, or could remove their spacesuits while on EVAs if they got too uncomfortable. Or some crews decided that 'suiting up' wasn't necessary for daily maintenance checks of water and power levels. Thankfully, all of us were in agreement on the parameters – we would remain on Mars until the arrival of Crew 174. That meant that every time we ventured outside, whether on an EVA, or conducting daily maintenance checks, our spacesuits would remain on us at all times. The only breach of this would be when running between the GreenHab, science dome and Hab. A series of dedicated tunnels between these sites had already been set up to allow for this breach anyway.

We also agreed on other terms for the mission: that we would only flush the toilet (once it had been unblocked) when we pooped and not when we peed; that any toilet paper we used would be put in a bag beside the toilet and emptied every morning; that to conserve water we wouldn't shower unless absolutely necessary – this was an easy one because the shower was filthy and caked in red mud. Before getting there, I had imagined that the 'not showering' rule would be a struggle for me, but already I was totally fine with it.

I was keen that we set up a cooking and cleaning schedule for the mission, which included pancake breakfast duties (for special days, including my dad's birthday the next day, Roy's mother's birthday on 24 January and Australia Day on 26 January) and preparing special meals from our countries on alternate evenings (i.e. the culture night dinners). We then went through the full fifteen Sols for which we would be on Mars and divided up daily duties of cleaning, lunch and dinner. I put the finalised rota on the fridge.

It felt as if we wanted to claim every inch of the facility as our own on that first Sol. We walked around each of the buildings and set up each space as we needed it. Then we began to chat about how we were going to tackle our first major objective of the mission – getting the toilet unblocked. I quickly found the toilet to be pretty disgusting, and flushing just for solids was tough. That stench of stale urine, knowing that it wasn't mine, would sometimes make me gag. Those first few days when the toilet was blocked were extremely stressful for us all. It was so early in the mission, at a time when we were still getting to know each other, so discussions around the blocked toilet were difficult. I mean, people still had to evacuate their bowels and bladder, so what were we supposed to do?

We contacted Shannon about it as in exceptional circumstances you can call in help from Earth, but she didn't believe that the situation required that level of assistance and had seen the toilet block many times before for other crews. She had left 'the snake' outside the Hab – a plumbing tool that is flexible enough to travel through the U-bend in the toilet, so that if there's a blockage further along the U-bend, you can use it to break it down. And fair play to Roy, he took the lead in trying to sort it out.

Shannon advised us not to use the loo until the issue was resolved, and to instead use plastic bags, which we could incinerate later on in a special section of the facility. I desperately needed to poo, but I didn't want to do it in the toilet and add to the disgusting mess that was already there. So I waited for everyone to be in the science dome, got a plastic bag and did my business in that, sealing the bag as quickly as possible. Within minutes the bathroom smelled badly. I panicked and wrapped it in a second bag. But the stench still filled the room. I grabbed the bag and left it in the engineering airlock. I was so embarrassed by the smell, but there were no windows to open.

I came clean with the crew the second they came back. They took it well. I was so relieved. I asked them how they were all managing their own situation. Some of them were still holding it in and were desperate to poo but didn't know what to do or how to poo into a plastic bag. I told them what I did, even demonstrating my squatting position. Roy had done the same as I had, so he chimed in on his preferred method. Soon we were in absolute hysterics. And that was the moment that I started to relax and properly bond with my crew. Pretty soon, we were calling the whole blocked toilet situation 'Poopgate'.

Two days later, the rain stopped and the toilet cleared itself. And Shannon got someone from Earth to come clear the sewage tank. I scoured that bathroom as best I could and while the toilet would block from time to time again during the mission, it was never for as long as those first few days, and, more importantly, it was never a difficult thing to discuss together as a crew.

***

But back to that first Sol. We spent the afternoon and evening unpacking, settling in and setting up our experiments. Michaela set up her indoor germination experiment in the main Hab downstairs. This was a Slovakian student experiment to compare the growth of spinach seeds grown under natural light and in soil with those under artificial light and fed with a solution seeded with nutrients. She planted her spinach seeds in the bespoke apparatus she had brought, designed by her students in Slovakia. While at MDRS, she would monitor the growth of the artificially lit seeds and Rick would monitor the growth of seeds planted in the GreenHab.

Meanwhile, Idriss and Roy worked on setting up their 3D printer. The plan was to print forty-one modular bricks and build a wall as proof of concept on the last Sol of our mission. However, after initial inspection of the 3D printer, they came across problems, namely that the filament spools at MDRS didn't seem to work. They then tried to heat up the extruder section of the printer to force the filament to go out, but not much progress was made on our first Sol on Mars.

Rick definitely adapted the best to our new environment and thrived in fulfilling his duties. On our first Sol, he monitored hourly the temperatures of the GreenHab, the lower floor of the Hab, and the grow tent in the GreenHab. He also took an inventory of our spices, made us dinner that night and somehow found ingredients for baking bread. We had found our first decent cook of the crew, and it helped that he was someone who really enjoyed spending time preparing dinner.

I took some photos of everyone working for the daily report that I had to submit to CAPCOM. I wrote a witty account of the blocked toilet episode. Overall, it was a fun first Sol, getting used to my new life on Mars. We all headed to bed around 10.30 p.m. My stuff was unpacked and I had found a place for all my items in my tiny state room, which measured something like 1.5 metres by 2.5 metres. I slept on top of a box-shaped mattress, which took up over half the room. The placement of the bed meant that I had a narrow passage to the back of the room, where there was a seat, a table and two shelves.

In terms of the order of the rooms, from left to right, there was Rick, me, Idriss, Roy and Michaela (she had a porthole in her room because she was the commander). Each room was more or less the same size. Everyone closed their door that night and settled down to some quiet time alone to reflect on the day.

I closed my eyes and tried to get to sleep, but the noise of the Hab made it difficult. Because it was winter at MDRS, the heating was on all night to protect us from the bitter sub-zero temperatures outside. It's a propane heating system that blows hot air via ducts into each of the rooms. It's noisy and makes the air very dry. I soon realised that if I closed my room door I would have no ventilation. So I got up and left my narrow door ajar slightly to allow fresh air to circulate. It didn't work well, though, and so I regularly woke up during the night gasping for air.

At one point, someone emerged from their room and headed to the toilet. And flushed (must have needed to poop then). The honking water motor kicked in directly beneath me for a full five minutes until the toilet cistern refilled. I realised that I had made a bad choice in my room selection. Sleep was going to be a luxury while on Mars.

Chapter 13

The Daily Grind on Mars

We got into a daily routine pretty quickly: up at 7 a.m. and breakfast together, where we discussed the plans for the day. The day went very fast at the Mars Desert Research Station. I had this imagined schedule in my head at the top of every day, thinking that there would be ample time to get all our tasks done efficiently, plus time to relax, chill out with the rest of the crew and rest up after dinner. But things would never go as planned. And I'm sure that's true for all MDRS crews. After all, you want to do so much to maximise your experience, aware that the mission and this opportunity to simulate living on Mars will be over before you know it. I wanted to do my own work *and* work with all the crew on each of their separate projects, *plus* capture the stunning landscape while on EVAs. In reality, that was far too much to fit into one Sol.

The Hab, and in fact the entire facility, was full of hard edges, cold steel, rust and dust. The best way to describe it is like trying to make a home out of your garage, complete with the WD40, and the space paint, mowers, tools and implements, and all the things you keep out of your house. Imagine then putting a kitchen table in the middle of that space, and cutting up the back wall into six rooms. That, in effect, is the best way to describe what it is like to live at MDRS.

But it makes sense, because if we are to attempt to colonise Mars, then this will likely be the only method of living there until a proper community is established. Just like the first pioneers of any new land, you live humbly and without comfort. And that's exactly how it felt for me at MDRS.

The weather became an integral part of our experience and it would be the first thing that we checked every morning. Cold, dry days were best. They meant that the ground remained relatively firm underfoot, so our boots wouldn't sludge about in red mud every time we left the Hab. Being caked in mud was kind of our boots' standard condition, however, which made them very messy to get on and take off. The mud made them pretty smelly too, as there were pockets of sulphur-containing rocks in the vicinity. You could also slip and fall in mud when wearing that heavy suit, so we were constantly advised by CAPCOM of the need to be vigilant in those conditions.

I struggled with the sleep deprivation, getting about three to five hours of disturbed sleep each night and waking up dehydrated from the dry hot air pumped into my room. So at the top of every Sol, I put my boots on and headed outside to the observatory area to get some fresh air into my lungs. That usually cleared the head and if that didn't work, a few litres of hot water followed by about five cups of coffee usually cleared it. The tiredness was tough, though. Everything gets more difficult when you are tired.

Michaela would check in with each of us to see what we were focusing on. Overnight I would charge the GoPro cameras and my own equipment. Michaela also had her own camera. I would download everyone's photos and videos each day, catalogue them, clear the SD cards so that they were ready for the next Sol of photos. It would take me hours every evening, but this was my main responsibility and I took it very seriously. Often I would plan interviews with each member of the crew, check in with them on progress and see how they were feeling. No one ever really grumbled much; we all just got on with it.

There was also the altitude to contend with. Shannon told us of previous crews who suffered from severe altitude sickness throughout their entire mission. So compared with them, we were faring quite well. Adjusting to our diet of mostly freeze-dried food was also challenging. It was a salty diet and once we had got through the fresh produce that we bought at Bull Mountain, it soon became a stodgy diet, which often made us constipated. Who knew so many foods could be freeze dried? Freeze-dried cabbage, freeze-dried butter, freeze-dried raspberries – freeze-dried everything! And of course there was also a limited water supply. Every time you boiled the kettle or made coffee, you were watching the tank. It was all part of adjusting to life on Mars.

***

Throughout the day we would either continue with the experiments or, if we had an EVA planned, we would get the gear together and head down to the suiting-up area near the main airlock.

EVAs were without doubt the best and most challenging part of my experience at MDRS. We had received training from both Crew 172 and from Shannon, so we all had the theory part down. But you can read about things, watch other people doing things and be told things, or even learn things, but nothing compares to actually doing it yourself.

It's a long slow process, preparing to go out on an EVA. You get slightly better at it the more you do it, but you always need assistance from your crew. First, you need clearance from CAPCOM that you can proceed. That involves putting in a request the evening before, during the daily communication (comms) session. Once you get the all clear from CAPCOM, you can begin procedures. Those not heading out on the EVA would assist the EVA team in suiting up. No more than three of us could head out on an EVA together, as it was a requirement for two crew members to remain at the Hab and monitor radio comms at all times, until the EVA team returned. The maximum amount of time allowed on one EVA was four hours.

To suit up, we stepped into the airlock section wearing our flight suits. We made sure that we were wearing enough layers of clothing underneath the flight suit to stay warm when we were outside, but not too many that we'd get too warm, as the temperature sometimes rose up to eighteen degrees Celsius in the afternoon. The external layer of clothing should really be a spacesuit. If we were actually living on Mars, of course this would be a suit with many layers of protection, something similar to the spacesuits worn by astronauts on board the International Space Station when they head out on EVAs. Mars is a treacherous place, after all; it's cold, windy and the atmosphere is thin, containing mainly carbon dioxide. Plus you're exposed to a lot more radiation from space on Mars than on Earth. But at MDRS, instead of wearing the actual spacesuit, we donned our flight suits instead. We also wore caps to keep our hair out of the way and to secure the radios. We each wore a headset for the two-way radio system. Once the radios were attached we did sound checks, making sure that the battery was fully charged and we were all set to the right channel.

Next up was the heavy air circulation unit worn across our back much like a rucksack. It's a fan system that was supposed to ventilate your helmet during the EVA. But a lot of these ventilation units weren't functioning properly. They were made of various sizes to match the needs of each crew. Based on our size, we were each assigned one of these units, which were numbered. There were six packs in total, but only four worked properly. I was assigned pack number four, which I shared with Idriss, as it was the best fit for us both. Wearing this backpack for up to four hours could be very uncomfortable, however, and if the fit was too tight or too loose, it got really sore on the back, shoulders and neck. But we made it work.

Lastly, once everything else was in place, we put on the

helmets. This was the most difficult part of it all. Like in scuba diving, the helmet was very uncomfortable to wear. Once secured in place with a series of clasps and fixtures, I felt isolated, shut off from everyone, my only means of contact being the two-way radio system. A feeling of claustrophobia often rose in me. Visibility was also limited and even more so when the ventilation pack wasn't functioning properly. The helmet fitted in such a way that I had to kind of crane my head forward a bit, and within a few minutes my whole shoulder and neck area would start to cramp up.

The first time we left the airlock to venture outside, I had a little moment. I now knew what this felt like. I would be able to make a decent stab at an EVA on Mars if I had to. And as long as I had an awesome team around me, I could survive it. That was reassuring to know.

Given that the crew were searching for soil and rock samples, they were keen to climb the hills and rock formations. Some were steep and some were mounds of red earth that appeared hard, but once we stepped on them, we realised that it was sandy underfoot. It is very difficult to keep your balance in the suit and if I climbed a steep incline the weight of the backpack made me feel like I was going to fall backwards if I didn't cling onto the rocks.

As someone with a fear of heights, it was terrifying at times for me to go out on these EVAs. But I was determined to keep up with the crew and so never discussed my fears. I didn't want to be viewed as the weakest crew member; I wanted to be just as capable as the rest of them. But it was a struggle at times. I would be gripped with fear, my heart beating fast, sweating in the cumbersome suit and carrying heavy camera gear with me, trying desperately to keep up with them. It was so frustrating to see others climbing capably ahead of me and me always having to pause, catch my breath and calm down in order to continue. My dear crew mates obviously realised that I had a fear of heights, but they never once spoke to me about it. If they saw that I was struggling to follow them up a difficult section, often times they came back and helped me climb, and we would reach the top together. The humiliation of those moments would almost make me cry. Trying to quash my pride and frustration, I let them lead me.

In return, I would take awesome pictures of them, and when back at the Hab, I completed my duties all the more effectively. I wanted to show my appreciation and respect for their protection of me when I needed it. And even when I was feeling down, I kept going, remaining in good form for them; cracking jokes, finding the funny moments to share whenever possible. Making them a hot cuppa when they would return from their EVAs. Helping them suit up and then disrobe post-EVA. Keeping the toilets pristine. Wherever I could do something to make my crew feel more comfortable, I did it. Because we all did that for each other. We all had our weaknesses and were a stronger team when we had each other's back.

As uncomfortable as wearing that suit was, it was always fantastic to go out on an EVA. It was the part of the mission that pushed us the hardest and was the most genuine off-Earth experience of the whole SIM experience. Without the EVAs it would have been an exercise in isolation. It was a unique experience, being an analogue astronaut. We take so much of our mobility for granted when we can wander aimlessly about nature, touching and photographing anything we want, for as long as we want. And, as I might have imagined, once I put my suit on, everything became difficult – simple camera tasks like being able to focus, choosing a frame size for a photo, clicking the shutter or altering the aperture – all of this was pretty much impossible with heavy gloves and a large glass visor between me and the eyepiece of my camera. Thankfully, I'd brought a really good wide-angle lens along with me, so once I selected my light settings, I was pretty set. But most of my shots were simply pot luck. With the beautiful light of the day, I struck gold on a few of them.

But photography aside, the experience was a special one for me as I got an opportunity to join my crew on their geological field trips, exploring, prospecting and sampling within the vicinity of our Hab. In my suit I gained a newfound respect for astronauts who have completed EVAs in space. Even though we were simply wearing a rucksack and a helmet around a desert, it gave me an appreciation and better understanding of the restrictions of space. If I was having difficulty moving about in what I was wearing, how difficult must it be for astronauts wearing those spacesuits? Where those suits are vital to their survival. If we fell in the suits while on EVAs, we would certainly hurt ourselves, but if we ripped our suits accidentally, it would be fine. If our helmets cracked, it would be a nuisance, but at least we could get up and continue our EVA. If any of those things were to happen to astronauts on Mars, then they would be in mortal danger.

As someone who genuinely wants to don a real spacesuit one day and become a participating member of a legitimate space mission, the EVAs brought me one step closer to that reality. I gained a real understanding of how much you have to rely on your support team to help you in and out of the suit, as well as how they remain in constant contact with you, and are there for you should anything go awry while you're outside the protection of the Hab.

***

Afternoons were usually quiet and calm. We would be off in our different areas of the facility, working away, and then, around 4 p.m., we would all start to gather again around the kitchen table to begin our daily reports. It would be snack time too, time for a hot water or tea or Tang with a few crackers or whatever snacks were left in the cupboard.

It was the most pressured part of the day for me, as the GoPros from the daily activities would be handed to me, filled with pictures and videos. The lads would be keen for a particular photo to be included in the creative report, so

I would quickly scan through everything and pull out any pictures that looked interesting. I was always trying to provide a variety every day, capturing the whole mission experience as best as I could. And then, after uploading all the content from the various SD cards of photos and videos, and editing a selection of them, I would need to get cracking on the creative report for the day. I was getting good at photographing the crew and their activities and they were keen to see what I had taken that day. I loved their enthusiasm for my work, but it would be tough sometimes to ask them politely to leave me alone for a few hours so that I could get the bloody daily report done.

Reporting was such a pain in the ass. CAPCOM would start comms at 7 p.m. and Michaela, as commander, would upload our reports to them, which would take a considerable amount of time due to the low bandwidth of the broadband at the facility. Comms would cease broadcasting after 9 p.m. If we had all our reports done by 7 p.m., then we could have a relaxing dinner together. But it was difficult to have the reports completed by 7 p.m.; in fact, it would often be just before 9 p.m. when the reports were submitted, especially if we had undertaken a long EVA.

Once I got my five photos and daily report done, I would give it to Michaela and carry on with the other tasks. Often Michaela liked to have input on the final selection of photos, and as commander it was her right to do so. It was those little things that occasionally irked me though, as I felt that this was one of the few duties that I had been given and that I was always very fair in making a balanced selection each day, reflecting all the crew's activities. I would sometimes take it personally, as if my capabilities were being questioned. Such little battles have the potential to escalate when you're tired and already have so little autonomy. I would do my very best to be mature and try to communicate my issues respectfully, but sometimes instead I'd give back with attitude, even ignoring Michaela at dinner. It was silly stuff that I'm not proud of. Those were my struggles.

***

We got a delivery of water on Sol four so we treated ourselves to our first shower in six days (except for Roy, who was the hardcore outdoorsy type of the crew). It was agreed that the guys would shower first while Michaela and I would wait until after them. Even though the shower area was dingy and pretty disgusting, it still felt amazing to step under the shower head and let a few dribbles of lukewarm water fall on my body. I didn't wash my hair, though, as that would have taken too long and wasted far too much water. It was probably a five-minute shower, but what a luxury. However, the most interesting part of the experience was realising afterwards how good I smelled. Which meant that we all must have smelled pretty rank prior to our showers.

It was funny how many of the rules and social norms of Earth didn't apply there. It was strange, but even after a few days at the MDRS, our lives back on Earth seemed a lifetime away.

Roy went looking for something in his room on Sol five and came across some US currency and brought it out to show us. Only days ago, back on Earth, we couldn't do anything without money. Breakfast $10. Batteries $4. Coffee to go $3. Now we could do nothing with it. Except perhaps rub some mud off our boots as we re-entered the airlock after an EVA.

That was one of the most interesting things about being a part of this SIM. When I'd stripped my daily routine back to simply surviving in the elements and completing daily tasks, life got a whole lot easier. And I couldn't help but reflect on life back on Earth. And all the stuff. The hoards of books that I probably hadn't opened in years, the wardrobe of clothes, shoes, and odds and sods, bed linen, towels, carpets, cushions, throws, scented candles, bicycles, houses, cafes, office blocks, buses, trains. All useless here.

High-value products on Mars include thermals, boots, camera, Internet, ATVs, heat, the solar generator, water, a functioning toilet, food, chocolate and coffee. Lots of coffee. Also tinfoil to cover our plates at mealtimes and cut down on washing up, movie night, sunrises, sunsets, the spice drawer, laughter, sharing stories, the crew – those things had become our currency.

***

On Sol ten we had a visit from aliens – from France, on Earth. Laurent and Jacques were two journalists from the French television station FR2. We got super-self-aware when they arrived, all of us whispering together about what we should do, how to act naturally, what we should say. We had already lost our socialising skills. It was a real struggle conversing with them. But of course Jacques and Laurent were lovely men, who were probably more out of their comfort zone than we were, having driven all the way out to the middle of the desert to meet us.

It all seemed to go very well. They filmed us at work in the GreenHab and science dome and then in the communal area. I was editing for most of the morning on my computer so was fortunate to be out of the way for the majority of their filming. But then they arrived in the communal area, where I was based, as Rick was making lunch. Both of us desperately tried to remain as natural and nonchalant as possible, even with the camera stuck in our faces. I quickly realised that everything I was saying seemed staged, way too energetic and completely out of character.

Jacques and Laurent shared lunch with us, which was freeze-dried gumbo. From a packet. Its sounds exotic, but this version of gumbo is essentially a big bag of 'Cup-a-Soup' with rice. Over lunch, Jacques and Laurent participated in some of the outreach work we did for our online followers. I had brought a special postcard with me from Ireland. It was kind of a 'scratch 'n' sniff' card, which had been seeded with all the volatile compounds that were detected on the surface of the comet 67P, which had recently orbited the Sun (ESA's wonderful Rosetta spacecraft had captured it all for us). The image on the card is an artistic impression of the comet created by Ekaterina Smirnova. Karen O'Flaherty, working at ESA ESTEC and particularly interested in supporting artists, asked me to ask the crew what we thought the card smelled like. So as we chewed on our salty gumbo, we passed the card around and each of us described what we thought the card smelled like.

Afterwards, Idriss, Roy and Michaela headed out on an afternoon EVA with Jacques and Laurent following behind, awkwardly acclimatising to the weird and limiting sensation of wearing the 'spacesuit'. Rick and I stayed in the Hab on radio duty.

When they all returned, Jacques and Laurent wouldn't come back upstairs. Instead they sat in the engineering bay, which seemed very strange to us. I made them coffee and dropped it down to them, but they didn't drink it. I caught them looking at each other as I climbed the stairs back to the communal area. It was then that I realised how everything must seem to them. And to the rest of the world. It was probably something like how Crew 172 had seemed to me on that first Sol here, only ten Sols ago, but a lifetime away. Jacques and Laurent likely felt that our lovely little Hab was filthy and unhygienic. We had become used to smelling, drinking bad coffee and eating salty, constipating food. And living together in this tiny space in the middle of nowhere.

We waved them off, inwardly relieved that they were gone. It had been weird having new people join us. They had invaded our lovely bubble and reminded us briefly that there was a whole other world just ten miles away from us. We weren't ready for that just yet. We had another three full days of beautiful isolation left to savour. Then we could worry about the rest of the world.

***

When you are confined in a tight space with the same people for two weeks, no matter how well you get along, it is going to test even the best of relationships. We had been very lucky; we all respected each other and knew when to step away to cool down. But there were moments when you would be prepared to do ten rounds in a boxing ring over who hadn't washed up properly, or who ate up all the broadband coverage.

I'm a reasonably laid-back person, usually, and in team situations my motto is to always put the needs of others ahead of my own. So when I saw any acts of selfishness going on, I struggled to keep my mouth shut. My other trigger is seeing someone taking advantage of their power, so again when I noticed some of the crew seeking special privileges because of their rank in the group, I would really struggle. At those times I would leave the group and rationalise that sometimes people aren't aware of their behaviour, or that differences in culture might be at fault.

It didn't help that there was little or no privacy on the mission. Our 'state rooms' were not a pleasant space to hang out in. My room in particular was not a restful place. The lack of personal space and time to myself were my biggest enemies on the mission. And not having a strict schedule for the completion of my own art project was a concern. For that, I just needed to keep thinking.

***

A key part of our mission at MDRS was to connect with the general public and schools, to tell a more human story about space, using our shared experiences as analogue astronauts. And, thankfully, we all shared a common passion for that part of the mission.

Roy had been requested to speak with some students on Earth. After a series of comms tests he obtained a secure connection (with the required time delay of twenty-two minutes between comms of course, to simulate the reality of the distance between Earth and Mars) and spoke with students from the Young Israeli Astronaut Academy, a programme that is part of the Davidson Institute of Science Education, the educational arm of the Weizmann Institute of Science in Israel. The students were interested in discussing the geological experiments with Roy, including the 3D printed bricks and regolith (soil samples collected while on EVAs) they were to be filled with. They also spoke to Rick and Idriss about their participation in the project.

We also took a call from French students who attended the same school that Idriss had gone to. We even spoke with his old English teacher, Mrs Magalie. They asked us all about our experience, from the experiments we were doing, to our daily lives while simulating Mars.

Michaela spoke with a Slovakian radio channel and we chimed in a little bit too with that interview.

And I continued to make short videos to answer questions that kept pouring in on social media. I made a point of uploading fresh content every day to Facebook to keep people up-to-date on our activities, even though it was a pain in the ass. Even using the lowest file sizes that I could, it would still take me at least two hours every night to complete uploading all the material. It was so frustrating, but I was determined to get it done. It sometimes meant waiting until everyone else was asleep and offline, sometimes as late as 1 a.m., but I would still do it. I knew that I wasn't going to get much sleep anyway. I was willing to do whatever I had to do to complete my daily tasks.

Chapter 14

Returning to Earth

The evening of Sol thirteen, our last evening at MDRS, was almost identical to our first evening. Except this time, we were on the other side of the table. We spent the morning finishing off our experiments and outreach activities. We gave the Hab a thorough clean and soon it was time for Rick and Idriss to go and pick up Crew 174 at Bull Mountain Market. Just like Patrick and Anushree had done for us two weeks earlier, which now seemed like a lifetime ago.

Once Crew 174 arrived – a seven-person crew from India – we took them through the Hab, telling them about the procedures to follow, how to suit up, how to go through the daily checks, how to monitor the water reserves, what to do if the toilet blocks and we even told them about using tinfoil to cover the plates.

Our packed suitcases were back on the ground floor near the engineering airlock, ready for our departure in the morning. We were no longer in SIM, which meant that we could venture outside without the cumbersome helmet and oxygen pack. Or boots. I could run up hills again, and go anywhere I wanted on the ATVs. We were all slightly skittish at the thought that we were going to be back on Earth soon. I started fantasising about pancakes and bacon and heaps of coffee. On crockery without tinfoil. As we got more animated, you could tell that Crew 174 thought we had gone stir crazy. We were probably just as feral as Crew 172; apparently, that's what happens after a mere fifteen days of isolation.

In hindsight, we were a crew that laughed a lot. We shared a sense of humour, which was an innocent one, often based on finding a series of phrases or sounds that we all enjoyed saying to each other. For example, the way Roy could mimic the sound of a peacock to perfection. We would plead with him repeatedly to do it for us, as it would crack us up so much. His peacock sound became our morning alarm to come to breakfast. And then our dinner alarm across the radio, as some of us would be in the science dome or GreenHab. And then he would do it just for laughs across the radio at random times.

Imagine that you were alone in the science dome, working away, and some of us were in the GreenHab or the main Hab or on an EVA. It could get pretty quiet. That's why we were always in radio communication. If you were lonely, or just wanted to check in with each other for no reason other than to just connect, those sorts of sounds, like the peacock call, were the perfect solution. So that's how we often ended up communicating by the end of our mission. As we came closer to the end of the mission, we became more nostalgic, and those sounds became even more significant to us.

I can only imagine how that all appeared to Crew 174 on their first day at MDRS with us, watching a bunch of us laugh hysterically as we would repeat sounds to each other. Yes, we had become feral, and yes, we had a severe case of cabin fever. But I think it's safe to say that we all loved it!

***

We lit a fire outside later that night to burn some rubbish and other odds and ends lying about the Hab. It was nice sitting outside, around the fire, on that bitterly cold night. Idriss took out his laser pointer and treated us to a stargazing session, pointing out stars we hadn't seen before, sharing distances and sizes and all sorts of delicious facts. We just lay on the ground around the fire, watching the stars and listening to Idriss. Content in that moment.

As the burning embers began to fade, we headed inside for our last night. My last night in that stuffy room of hot dry air. As I was lying there (NOT sleeping, as ever), I had mixed feelings about leaving in the morning. Sure, I was looking forward to seeing everyone again and enjoying the spoils of living in actual houses with fresh food. But I was also sad. I had lived a very simple life at MDRS. I had wanted for nothing, because there had been nothing to want! I had everything I needed, and while it was basic, I was really comfortable living meagrely. I wondered how I would adjust to being back on Earth.

Roy had suggested that we get up to watch the sunrise together, so at 7 a.m. we all tapped gently on each other's walls, trying not to wake Crew 174, who were still asleep in the communal area. Once outside, we climbed the nearest hill and watched the Sun come up. Our final act as Crew 173 at MDRS.

When we got back inside, Crew 174 were up and making breakfast. In our kitchen. Around our table. But of course none of it was ours any more. Shannon returned to the Hab to check that everything was in order. She told us that in all her years of managing MDRS, she had never met a happier crew. She had listened in on radio communications in case of emergency and loved our banter across the radio waves.

The handover complete, we packed the SUV with our gear and waved goodbye to Crew 174. Michaela, Idriss, Rick, Roy and I were now officially back on Earth and I wasn't sure how I felt about that.

**

It was about 8.30 a.m. when we headed into the only open diner, Brenda's Diner, in Hanksville. As planned, I ordered pancakes with heaps of coffee. Delicious. Time to use money again too. Roy and Michaela took the map out and planned our last day together – we decided on a road trip to Canyonlands National Park about eighty miles away. I went to the loo just before leaving. I noticed how spotless it was.

As I walked out of the cubicle, I remembered that I was no longer at MDRS and so probably needed to flush the toilet. It seemed nonsensical to me, to flush a perfectly clean toilet containing probably about 200 millilitres of my urine. But I knew that I was back on Earth now and so needed to comply with courteous and considerate behaviours here. So, in the end, I flushed the toilet. And it flushed for so long, using way too much water for my meagre 200 millilitres. It seemed ridiculous to me; for a moment, I half-thought that I had somehow broken the cistern. But I hadn't. I was appalled by the waste.

Then I washed my hands and again, as I turned on the tap, water came gushing out. So I quickly turned if off as I lathered my hands. I had become used to globules of water slowly emerging from those noisy honking taps at MDRS, pushed through the pipes by way of a very inefficient and small pump. I had managed well enough to keep myself clean for over fifteen days with that minimal amount of water.

When I returned to the table, it turned out that all of us had come to the same conclusion on our bathroom trips.

We all gathered our things and headed back to the truck. Roy was gazing back at the diner in contemplation. I asked if he was okay. 'I'm not sure,' he said. 'Its all been so easy for the past few weeks. We had everything we needed and I'm not sure that I want to get used to all this luxury again.'

I knew what he meant. I mean, the diner was by no means luxurious, but compared with where we had just come from, it was practically paradise. It all seemed so indulgent, so easy. I didn't want to get soft again. I had learned how to survive successfully and happily with a life stripped back to the bare essentials. And I'd liked it. I hadn't expected that to happen.

***

We had an awesome afternoon together in Canyonlands, with Roy and Michaela telling us about the geological features of the stunning national park that ranged in age from the

Permian to Cretaceous periods (yes, I had learned lots from my crew mates!).

Then it was time to go our separate ways. Roy and Idriss were the first to leave; they were travelling to Los Angeles. So we all hugged, said goodbye and that was that. Roy had been the peacemaker of our group, and probably the most knowledgeable person. Whenever I was overwhelmed or in need of calm, I would find Roy and Rick and just sit with them in silence. We never spoke about how we were feeling, as we knew the detrimental effect that it would have on the group bond. We had all signed up for this experience, after all, and so we each had to deal with our own personal demons and triggers. Complaining about it to the crew would only make matters worse, so out of respect for each other, we chose to keep our complaints and frustrations to ourselves and use the time alone – or, for me, sitting in silence with Roy and Rick – to reflect and bounce back.

I had been dreading saying goodbye to Roy all day. He had shared so much of himself on our mission. He told us about his life in the kibbutz and his mother, as well as the traditions of his life. He had brought a pack of 'Go Fish' cards that had been made in the kibbutz. We played it every night. As we turned each card, all with different illustrations, he would tell us the story about that illustration. He even taught us how to read Hebrew – Rick picked it up really quickly, but me? Not so much. He would get so upset if there were any tensions in the group. He was the father of the group, without a doubt.

With Idriss and Roy's departure, Crew 173 would be no

more. I had spent seventeen days in total in the company of these people since that first morning at the Days Inn, rarely alone for the entirety of that time, so the thought of us all going our separate ways was breaking my heart.

So we began our goodbyes. I first hugged Idriss and thanked him for his friendship and care. And then it was time to say goodbye to Roy. I didn't want to cry so we hugged for a long time, and so tightly, and patted each other on the back. I wanted to tell him that his friendship had gotten me through the mission and I couldn't thank him enough for everything. Sometimes words are just not enough, however, and that hug said more than anything I could ever have articulated. We separated, both in pieces. Rick grabbed me and nested me under his arm. As they walked away, Idriss ran back to give us all another hug; he was crying now. So was Michaela. We all were. No words needed to be exchanged. Then they got in the truck. Idriss opened the window and screamed out our 'peacock' sound. We laughed, waving them off. And then they were gone.

Michaela and I shared a room, with Rick in the room beside us, at the Days Inn, the same dingy place that I had stayed in that first night I arrived in Grand Junction. Michaela came out of the shower smelling magnificent, gushing about how exquisite the shower had felt. Boy, was she right! A proper shower. With hot water. I got to wash my hair too. I was so dirty that the water running off me had a dull brownish-red hue. I thought that I had kept myself pretty clean, but clearly I was mistaken.

I got out of the shower smelling gorgeous! I kept sniffing my hair and skin. And I put back on the clothes that I had travelled over to America in. They smelled beautiful too. All my clothes from MDRS now had a thick odour: a metallic, sulphuric and soil-based kind of smell. Scents of the land that surrounded MDRS.

We converged in an Applebee's restaurant across the road. I hardly recognised Michaela and Rick, dressed in real clothes and smelling so sweetly. Rick couldn't get over how smooth his beard was after a wash and trim. Michaela was travelling onward with two friends who had joined us at the restaurant. Again, I could see how weird we must have appeared to them. They seemed so subdued in comparison to the three of us.

We messaged Idriss and Roy with voice memos all night, leaving a few peacock squawks for them. Michaela headed to bed early as she was leaving first thing in the morning. I stayed up, however, as I'd promised Rick that I would get drunk with him. For those who know me, I'm not a drinker, but that night I made an exception. We hung out with the waiting staff from Applebee's and ended up in a local diner drinking hot chocolate. It was bizarre to feel so free.

I felt so much love for my crew that night; they were like my family now. I didn't want to go to bed; I wanted to hang out with Rick, my little brother of sorts. And I was dreading leaving him in the morning. I had drawn from his sense of calm a lot during the mission. He never got fazed by anything and I had always felt safer whenever he was around. So that night, drinking together, was kind of weird. I felt a whole mix of things – exhilaration for completing this huge mission together; giddy to be back in the real world, eating and drinking so many things that tasted so great; and then there was this outpouring of love for my crew, while also knowing that I would soon be without all of them. I wanted to say so much to them, but it was all too overwhelming. We had been through so much together. And now it was almost over.

**

I got up early the next morning to have breakfast with Michaela before she left. I gave her another huge squeeze of a hug and, between tears, thanked her again for doing such a great job as our commander. Then she was gone.

Rick was supposed to join us for breakfast but never showed. I headed over to the Wendy's near the motel to have breakfast and texted him. Again there was no word. I had wanted to spend the last few hours at Grand Junction hanging out with him, but now I realised that I'd be lucky to see him at all.

Soon it was time to check out of the Days Inn. I ran to Rick's room and after a few knocks he finally opened the door. I gave him a huge hug and ran out before he saw my tears.

Within minutes of leaving the hotel, I was already feeling so lonely. But this was going to be my life now and I needed to re-adjust back to that.

I got the Greyhound bus to Denver and then onward to New York. I had booked four days' holidays for myself there.

At the time of the booking, I had imagined that I would be in need of a nice mini-break before returning to Dublin. I had expected to be full of energy, as I usually am in New York, to go exploring and sightseeing and to soak up the fast pace and vibrancy of the city. But other than walking the Highline, a short jaunt around Central Park, hitting a launderette and a trip to MoMA, I did very little. My time there was instead spent in my hotel room, sleeping or sending everyone in the crew edited pictures and video clips. I also started to get really sick with flu, which further drained my energy and enthusiasm for going out exploring.

***

The response to our mission was pretty astounding. I hadn't expected much interest, but even the media in Ireland seemed keen to know about my adventure. This was largely due to Graeme Lennox from *The Sunday Times*, who had heard about the mission while I was away and conducted a long interview with me on our second-last Sol at MDRS (I broke my SIM to do it but didn't ask him anything about the world when he interviewed me).

The media storm broke in Australia first, as Rick arrived home before the rest of us. And since I had all the footage and photography, I had to prepare a pack of photos and videos for us all to distribute in each of our home countries. *National Geographic* did a feature on Roy, and I managed to get two of my images published in his article, something of which I'm especially proud.

I landed back in Dublin on the morning of my birthday, 5 February, at 5.30 a.m. When I switched on my phone, my crew mates' birthday wishes were the first ones I saw on my Facebook page.

Even though I was feeling pretty crap from the flu and long flights, it was lovely to be home. I was so excited to see the sea and hear the birds in my neighbourhood. I got off the Aircoach with my heavy case and raced to the sea front. It was still dark, but I could hear the waves. I stood there for a long time, just absorbing it all and inhaling all that lovely fresh air.

Then I walked back to my apartment. It seemed ENORMOUS, so much more luxurious than I remembered it. I realised that I had way too many possessions. I hadn't missed any of these things when I was at MDRS. With the exception of some small ornaments and pictures, I no longer had a personal connection with any of these items. I went and flushed my toilet. As I expected, there was too much water used per flush.

I had picked up a copy of *The Sunday Times* at the airport. Graeme had written a three-page spread about my mission, using the photos that I had taken (and some from Michaela too). He had even placed me on the front cover.

I slept for a few hours and when I got up I called Mam and Dad. They were so happy to hear that I was home safe. My friends had prepared a very small but special birthday dinner for me. There was so much to tell everyone, though I was still processing a lot of it myself. Emails started coming in that evening and all the next day, with requests to interview me for the radio or papers. Something had shifted regarding my journey to get to space. There was increased interest.

Pat Kenny interviewed me on Newstalk. My flu had worsened and I barely had a voice at that stage, but I still made sure to give the interview. After all, the main purpose of my mission was to spread the message of space to the general public. All those hours spent recording and uploading and downloading SD cards and editing and uploading to Facebook at MDRS were starting to pay dividends. The interest in the mission was exceptional in all our home countries and we all received requests to speak to the public. Even though some of our science experiments weren't successful, we had succeeded in the mission objectives that I had written out on St Patrick's Day a year earlier.

My Mars mission is still one of most talked-about aspects of my space journey so far. Two years on and I still include videos and images of Crew 173 at almost every talk I give. And the mission appeals to audiences of all ages and backgrounds. I hadn't expected the mission to have such a huge impact.

What made that mission so special was the group of people I was fortunate enough to share it with. I hit the jackpot when I was invited to be a part of Crew 173. I still keep in touch with my crew mates, maybe not as much as I did those first few months post-mission, but they are still close by. MDRS is a unique experience and going through it all together meant that we bonded on a deep level. Maybe it was because of how we always kept a watchful eye on each other while on EVAs, or the way we cooked for each other, or how we brainstormed in figuring out how to solve Poopgate. Or maybe it was all of it, experiencing it all together.

It really was an incredible adventure and something I'm very proud to have achieved. I hadn't expected to deal so capably with the harsh environment or the isolation. I had worried in advance about not showering and the lack of privacy. But I did just fine. The experience showed me that I could push myself much harder than I had expected. And that I wouldn't do too badly if I was put in the same situation again. Which is why I want to continue with isolation studies. Maybe a longer one the next time. It's all good preparation, should I ever get a place on an actual trip to Mars.

Chapter 15

Back to Earth

The week after returning from Mars, I began work on a new theatre show (which initially had the working title 'Hand in Space') with the help of Sarah Baxter, my director from *To Space*. I was so inspired by my Mars mission that it made sense to us both that we set the next show on Mars in the future, at a time when I had achieved my dream of getting to space. We set it in 2036, as if Elon Musk's prediction for the colonisation of our neighbouring planet had been put into practice. The characters in the show are scientists on a two-year mission to establish and test long-term colonisation parameters.

While on the analogue mission, I had often considered the work of all the people involved in putting one astronaut into space. I wanted to tell their story in this new show; the story of the unsung heroes, the people behind the scenes, their collective will and united purpose. With this in mind, I went on field trips to ESA's Astronaut Centre, where I interviewed about a dozen scientists, engineers, doctors and communicators who were all involved in some way with human-led missions. I also knew that I had to tell the story of the toil of space, the mundane and everyday aspects of exploration, the lack of glamour and sacrifices involved. Together Sarah and I pored over the interviews, grabbing snippets, trying to tie the story together.

During all this, I realised that my MDRS experience was inspiring me to look at my life differently. I saw how all the 'stuff' that I had gathered over the years was largely irrelevant to me. I was embarrassed that I had so many things. I also now valued water and energy differently, and that new outlook on natural resources had remained with me. I liked the feeling of possessing very little while at MDRS. It had allowed me to feel lighter and more focused.

Once back in my apartment, I decided to change the way I live in order to match the values and responsibilities I now had when it came to our planet and managing its resources. I looked at my wardrobe of clothes and, having survived on two pairs of trousers, four tops and underwear at MDRS, I knew that I could dispense with a lot of it. The books on my shelf too. I hadn't looked at many of them for years, so why were they still there? Surely they could be put to better use if I passed them on. And that's what I began to do. It has taken me some time to clear everything out – in fact, I'm still not finished – but since that Mars mission I've been consistently downsizing my life. My MDRS experience also inspired me to bring a stronger message about our relationship with planet Earth to my work.

Since 2016 Dad had been teaching me beekeeping, and while I was at MDRS I kept thinking about a community of bees, how they work together. So, when we went to make the show, I knew that beekeeping could add an interesting dimension to the show's story. And also a nod to my dad, a thank you of sorts for inspiring me to live a life led by my curiosity.

By the summer, the show was written. We called it *Diary of a Martian Beekeeper*. It premiered in Cork as part of Space Week 2017 and we had a run in March 2018 at Smock Alley in Dublin, gaining fabulous reviews.

***

In addition to making *Diary of a Martian Beekeeper* in 2017, I was also involved in putting together the core lectures for the Space Studies Program that would be hosted in Cork, at Cork Institute of Technology (CIT), and also at Blackrock Castle Observatory, where I was still the artist in residence.

As well as weekly calls with Geoff Steeves and Chris Welch, who co-chaired the core lectures (I was their associate chair), which meant putting in at least ten hours a week for this segment of the SSP17 programme, I also worked closely with Blackrock Castle in providing a series of public events for the local Cork community. With so many leading experts on many space-related topics coming to Cork, it seemed ridiculous for us not to roll out our own separate programme of public events. Clair McSweeney at Blackrock Castle and Niall Smith, Elizabeth Twomey and their team at CIT did an awesome job on the ground, working with Omar Hatamleh, the new director of SSP17 (and successor to John Connolly), and his team in bringing the whole programme together for June 2017. Juggling my time between trips to ESA's Astronaut Centre, planning core lectures and public events for SSP17 and writing the theatre show meant that my plate was very full. But I loved it all; I knew how fortunate I was to have so many space activities in my life. I wasn't going to take it for granted.

I more or less moved down to Cork for the summer, staying at the SSP residence at Deans Hall in Bishopstown. And once the Space Studies Program kicked off that first week after the opening ceremony, we got into our groove, delivering a good standard of core lectures for that year's participants. I was particularly delighted to have the opportunity to give two of the space humanities lectures in communications and the arts.

It was important to Chris, Geoff and I that we spent time with all the lecturers who had been invited on campus and we went to great lengths to ensure that they felt welcome. And in my capacity as artist in residence for Blackrock Castle, I also assisted Niall and Liz on the ground, acting as host for participants as well as the SSP staff, chairs and visiting faculty. It was important to us all that they experienced the 'Irish welcome', so I took the time to show many of our guests around Cork and its environs. Whatever was required, I was happy to help out. It meant that I would stay on site long after core lectures ended, but that wasn't such a bad thing. I had met and hung out with many of the visiting lecturers the previous summer in Haifa. It was lovely to see them all again and I was delighted to show them around the city. They were kindred spirits of sorts. It was a pleasure having the opportunity to spend time with them again.

In the middle of this already hectic schedule, the opportunity to speak at InspireFest about my dream to get to space arose. Ann O'Dea, founder of InspireFest, invited me to speak at this highly regarded annual event, created to promote STEM and inspire people to think outside the box. With a line-up of international and inspirational speakers, I had an opportunity to share the stage with them at the Bord Gáis Energy Theatre in Dublin in early July.

The timing wasn't perfect – unfortunately it was taking place right bang in the middle of our core lectures programme and my commitment for the summer was to SSP – but when I explained the importance of the opportunity to Omar, our SSP director, and to my core lecture co-chairs Geoff and Chris, they worked together to allow me to leave Cork and speak at this important event.

It was an opportunity to reach a new audience and extend the space community and network of friends who were already rallying behind me. And it was also a huge privilege to have been invited to speak amongst such highly respected game changers, influencers and outside-the-box thinkers; people who were making great strides in promoting STEM in their own areas of expertise.

I was very nervous about it but knew that if I could do a good job it would be a valuable experience. I was speaking in the early part of the morning, straight after Taoiseach Leo

Varadkar officially opened the event. I watched the Taoiseach address the audience in this intimidating theatre from the wings. I breathed deeply to remain calm, desperately keeping the first line of my speech in my mind. All too soon the Taoiseach finished, and as he walked past, he wished me good luck. And then it was my time to hit the stage and share my story, my mission, my quest.

I had a few slides to share, some footage of my Mars mission but, most importantly, footage of that day back in 2011 when I wore that ESA flight suit and this whole ambition of mine began in earnest. I walked slowly onto the stage, took a breath and looked at the audience for a couple of seconds. Then I began. 'Have you ever had a moment of clarity?' I asked them. And I shared my moment of clarity, explaining why it was important for me to go to space, to realise the dream of my eight-year-old self, to finally live the life that I felt destined to live.

I finished with 'My name is Niamh Shaw and I have this dream. And I'm going to achieve it.'

I walked off stage, thanked the tech team and, once I was alone, I had a massive cry. I had done it. I had made another massive leap forward in the dream. I was getting more comfortable reaching out, outlining my dream. Soon my Twitter feed started to go berserk with words of encouragement. My pals Orlaith and Clair from Blackrock Castle appeared. They were astounded by how well it had gone and we all celebrated the moment together. I couldn't have done it without Orlaith, who worked with me for hours on perfecting my speech, and having Clair there also helped me a great deal.

I needed to learn to ask for help more. I was starting to realise the importance of that if I was to have any chance of making this big space goal a reality. I know that being a part of InspireFest showed people that I was serious about my quest. Opportunities to speak at more events and schools and festivals emerged after that day, further opportunities for me to share my space adventures with a wider audience and, more importantly, spread the word as to what I was trying to achieve.

In addition to InspireFest, the opportunity to participate in a zero gravity flight just dropped into my lap that summer. Mexican artist Nahum, whom I had met the previous summer while attending SSP16 in Haifa, contacted me about a last-minute slot on a special charter flight that had become available. Earlier that year I had reached out to him online to ask about a previous zero gravity flight that he had done and how I could go about arranging one. Thanks to that chat, he approached me the minute he heard about this vacancy. I still had to pay for it, of course, but I reckoned that with consistent work now coming in I could just about afford to make it happen. And so Nahum introduced me to Andreas Bergweiler from Space Affairs, who was arranging the flight.

It would require me to get to Russia for five days in August.

Sarah was happy for me to adjust our rehearsal schedule, and I had no commitments that week at SSP17, so it was all systems go. Other than arranging flights and a Russian visa, I was ready to head to Star City, Moscow to finally experience the sensation of weightlessness.

I felt like I was taking another step closer to my dream.

Part 4

Lift Off

Chapter 16

Zero G

15 August 2017, 8 a.m.

I haven't been to my doctor to get the special motion sickness plasters, something that we can use to reduce the chances of vomiting during the flight. We had been advised to do this in our information pack, as well as eating a full breakfast the morning of the parabolic (or Zero G) flight.

I'm terrified. I'm once again completely out of my comfort zone, but that's exactly why I'm here, why I've decided to do this Zero G flight. I'm tired of having a list of things that I want to do, my 'bucket list' to experience, while never being bold enough to do anything about it. I'm in a new phase of life now, challenging this fear and exploring how I cope in extreme circumstances, and then documenting it all, whether good or bad. I'm working on a new art project on this very notion, and the Zero G experience is part of that – the idea of everyday people being put in extraordinary circumstances.

The travel group is quite intimidating, though. Half of them know each other already; they're the awesome team from 'Die Astronautin', a German initiative led by the lovely Claudia Kessler to get a German woman into space. The two final astronaut candidates from this programme are here – Insa Thiele-Eich and Nikola Baumann. They're impressive women, who are part of a very interesting mission. As are their support crew, Carmen and Laura, who are also finalists from that same initiative. And if that wealth of talent and expertise isn't intimidating enough, we also have the amazing Susi, a former Olympic ski champion who now specialises in indoor surfing. She's such an accomplished woman, quietly confident in her achievements, never bragging or dominating. I feel early on that I can rely on her if I need to, that she's keeping a protective eye on me from a distance. We get along very well from the moment we meet at the airport. And the more time I spend with her, the more I discover about the full life that she has lived. So wise, the real deal, the perfect role model for women of all ages. The kind of woman I want to be.

Galina is our guide and one of our translators on the trip. She was the very first person I met in Russia, meeting me off the plane. I was nervous entering Russia, especially going through passport control. And I wasn't sure how safe it would be to travel solo to Moscow, so it was a relief to see her. It felt like we immediately got along and I am really enjoying her company. Then there's Norbert from Hungary, Rok from Slovenia, Matthias from Germany and the sweet and gentle Mannfred, a doctor and paramedic for mountain expeditions.

Lastly there's Kalle and Mazdak from Space Nation, Finland. We bonded the day before, at the Gagarin Research and Test Cosmonaut Training Center (GCTC), in the corridor outside the doctor's office. As we waited for our medical exam to give us the all clear for the flight, we got a fit of giggles, probably from nerves (certainly for me) or from the realisation of where we were and what we were about to do. They are a cheeky duo, keen to explore areas of Star City – the training centre for cosmonauts – beyond the boundaries in which we have been confined. Apologising with a smile whenever they get rumbled. I really like them. I like people who are impish and bold, but in an innocent way. They are driven by their curiosity and are outsiders. Like me. Mazdak is a filmmaker and artist too, so we have lots in common: shared values, a shared desire to inspire and a shared hope to bring our passion for space to all. This is also the core aim of their company, Space Nation.

Kalle adopts a protective role over a sub-group of us, whenever we get separated from the 'Die Astronautin' group (who have a separate itinerary from us, at times). He takes the lead, in a gentle way, when we tour the GCTC to the centrifuge, the Soyuz, Mir and ISS training modules. And during any other instances when we were separated from the bigger 'Die Astronautin' group. We have all found our roles in this sub-group. I like the group a lot; they all know what I'm trying to do while at Star City and are keen to help me in any way they can.

On the morning of the actual Zero G flight, I feel the least qualified of the bunch. It is as if everyone else on the flight knows a lot more than me, that they are better used to being out of their comfort zone. So I'm quiet on the bus journey to the runway. Susi engages me in chat a few times, though, keeping an eye on me, which is nice.

We stop outside Star City to collect our translator, Lena,

and take a bunch of photos together. No one is talking about what we're about to do. We're all excited, and equally nervous, though we are not sharing our fears. I'm wearing my Crew 173 flight suit from the Mars mission; it feels appropriate to wear it for this flight.

A bigger bus arrives; it's the support team from the GCTC, who will be taking care of us during the flight. We had met some of them the day before during the Zero G training. I sit beside one of them. He has no English and I have no Russian, so we simply smile at each other a lot.

Andreas from Space Affairs, who has arranged the trip, is all business. This is the day. This is the reason why we're all here, so he probably feels that pressure, I'm sure. He has generously allowed me to bring my own GoPro onto the plane, even though he already has a network of cameras rigged up on the plane; it is all so I can capture this experience for my own art project. We have spoken extensively about my work and the importance of this Zero G flight in what I'm trying to achieve. Andreas understands artists and wants to support me, to help me capture what I need. It calms me, makes me feel less pressured among this impressive group and reminds me that my purpose on this trip is different: to absorb the experience, to document it, whether good or bad. I remember that I've already prepared myself for all outcomes, and if this flight doesn't go well for me, I want to know that, one way or another. I want to capture it as much as I would a successful flight. As long as I record my experience, then it's a success. That's why I haven't brought the special anti-emetic plasters. I don't need to be the expert; I'm the everyday person, putting myself in an extreme situation to see how I get on. But it's difficult to remember all this in the moment, with all the excitement, absorbing the energy of these capable people, who all want to excel in Zero G.

***

The bus pulls up outside the Ilyushin plane and we all get out. Everyone is excited. We take pictures and explore the plane, inside and out. The flight is imminent now. I'm excited and terrified but regretting that I didn't get those special anti-emetic plasters. We've been told again by the GCTC lead about the possibility of vomiting, and what to do in this instance. It's a very real possibility.

I climb into the plane, the interior of which is huge. I set up my GoPro at the back of the plane, a distance away from the main group, which will give me the space to do what I need to do. I also have my zoom voice recorder and my DSLR. I place all my other equipment in a nearby pouch – my Lottie doll, my young supporter Hayden's painting and a poster for the theatre show *Diary of a Martian Beekeeper*.

Yesterday, we were taken through training for the parabolic flight. We will have ten manoeuvres in total, that's ten segments of Zero G, each lasting an average of forty seconds. The first manoeuvre, we are told, is a short test phase, to allow us to get used to the sensation. For the second manoeuvre, we will all link arms together as a group. I've assigned tasks for myself for the next five (flying with Hayden's painting, flying with my Lottie doll and floating the theatre poster) and then, once I have footage of these activities, I can devote the last three manoeuvres to simply enjoying the experience.

Everyone has found his or her spot now. Kalle has taken the spot beside me. A cosmonaut in training is directly across from me, up at the back of the aircraft. Beside him is Mazdak. Norbert is beside Mazdak, and Rok is beside him. Markus, the photographer, is then beside Rok. I can't see who is beside Kalle; I think it's Mannfred, but I'm not sure. The 'Die Astronautin' team are at the front of the plane; I can't really see what they're up to. I do know that, like me, they have tasks to achieve during most of the ten manoeuvres. I imagine that their camera team has a lot going on, so I'm glad that I'm a distance away from them. I can focus on what I need to do, without getting in their way.

One of the GCTC team approaches me and assists me in putting on the heavy parachute. It's difficult to move once it's attached, it's so heavy, heavier than other parachutes I've worn before, and it's restricting my movements. The GCTC lead calls us together, so I manage to stand up and waddle towards him for his final briefing before take-off. Our translator, Lena, shares his last-minute instructions in English. The engines are running and it's very difficult to hear her so I get as close as I can. The lead goes over again what's going to happen. He reminds us of what he covered the day before during training, then gives us all two plastic bags. We take them and don't need Lena to explain their purpose to us. We all know what they're for, and all hope that we will not need them. If we vomit, it's our responsibility to take care of it. We're then instructed to lie on the soft cushioned floor and await further instruction.

I press record on the GoPro and the voice recorder. And we're off! The plane is in the air.

It feels like we're in the air for a really long time before anything happens. I enjoy the opportunity to lie on the cushioned floor of a plane. It's a really nice place to be. I take a look to my left. Kalle is smiling. It's too noisy to even try to speak. So instead we exchange a thumbs up. I look across at Mazdak and we smile and exchange another thumbs up. Then Markus and I exchange a thumbs up. It feels like the calm before the storm.

I look up at the ceiling, at the bright lights. We've been told to keep an eye on the lights, that they will brighten once we are about to begin the 2G phase. This means that we will begin to feel the 2G force on our bodies, which will make us feel very heavy. This phase will last for about twenty seconds. Then we will enter the Zero G phase. We have been warned that we will hear an announcement on the tannoy from the GCTC team when it's safe to move in Zero G; we are not to move before that announcement. The Zero G phase will last about thirty seconds. There will be a GCTC team member nearby, keeping an eye on us, to help us familiarise ourselves with how to move safely when in Zero G. We must follow their instructions, so when they tell us to go to ground, we must do it. We must already be on the ground when the lights dim. Because the second phase of 2G will be coming, for another twenty seconds, as we exit the parabolic manoeuvre. And no one should be moving in 2G, as that's when the vomiting sensation will come.

I start to feel a change in the mood of the GCTC team. I notice that they are preparing for something. My nearest GCTC guy, Peter, taps me on the shoulder and instructs me to hold on to the bar, which runs the whole length of the plane at about hip height. I pull myself up from my lying position on the floor to a seated position and lean against the wall of the plane, holding the bar. Kalle and I exchange another look; he's beaming back at me. So are Mazdak, Norbert and Rok. Here we go; it's all about to kick off!

The lights change and a bizarre sensation fills my body. It slowly starts to feel heavier and heavier, and I especially feel it in my head – an increasing dull pressure that immediately makes me feel queasy. My initial response is to move, to shake off the sensation, but I've been told that this is the worst possible thing to do. So instead, I decide to go completely limp in my body and let the sensation happen to me, rather than trying to fight it. It goes against all my survival instincts to do this, but once I go limp I immediately feel better. So I stay very still as this bizarre sensation works through my body.

The voice comes through the tannoy and the lights get very bright. I'm still feeling this heavy feeling in my body, but Peter, my GCTC guy, gestures for me to move my body. I gently push myself up and then I don't really know what's happening. I can't figure out where my legs are in relation to my arms; it feels like I'm in a swimming pool, holding on to the bar. I'm somehow floating but am in a state of confusion as to why or how it's happening. I don't know how to move my body when I'm floating, everything feels topsy-turvy. I find the sensation both hilarious and kind of scary, much like the way rollercoasters make me feel. There is some bizarre force of nature acting on my body, which I've never felt before, and I absolutely love it. I start to laugh and scream, loving the energy and chaos of what's going on.

I look at everyone around me and see we're all finding our own way of figuring it out. We all seem equally hesitant, but there are also lots of smiles. Then the lights go dim and Peter is tapping my shoulder to get down. I descend back to the floor and let my body go limp as that heavy 2G pressure returns to my body. And it immediately makes me feel queasy. I'm worried that I'm going to vomit, so I relax my body more.

The lights go back to normal and the 2G sensation leaves. I sit up on the ground and look around at everybody. We're all beaming and laughing and giving a thumbs up to each other. I can see that I'm a lot more energised than others about it. I start to punch the floor and scream and laugh. I feel amazing and can't wait for the next session of Zero G.

The sequence is so unique; I love the whole experience. I enjoy the confusion, the liberty it brings to my body, the fact that I'm constantly trying to make sense of what's happening. My brain is in overdrive, trying to compare this experience to previous experiences, and when it cannot, the geography of my body gets completely lost in my mind. Being in that state of confusion is such a liberating sensation. It's something that can only be understood in the experience, in the moment. It's kind of like swimming in water, but there's no resistance in any way when you try to move.

I loved my Zero G flight. Every single moment, even the 2G pressure on the body. The whole experience taught me a lot about myself, as well as about my body. Everyone around me had their own personal experience, and I don't think any of them are comparable. For me, I held on to the bar for the majority of my Zero G manoeuvres, and only realised that I had done that about twelve hours later. I certainly wasn't the most aerodynamic or adventurous participant on the flight, but it was an extraordinary experience – challenging at times but, as a consequence, hugely rewarding.

Seemingly, I laughed and screamed for nearly every manoeuvre (which I wasn't aware of – my screaming pretty much killed any chance to use audio of the flight – sorry!). Peter stayed with me throughout each manoeuvre and would tell me how many rounds of Zero G were remaining. He helped me with all my activities: getting Hayden's painting to float, flying with Lottie, he even carried me at one stage to allow me get my theatre poster to float across my GoPro lens. On the last lap, we shook hands and he helped me fly across the width of the plane, pushing me gently into doing something new for the final lap of my Zero G flight.

And then it was over. We were done. Two hours had passed in the blink of an eye. I gave Peter a huge handshake and thanked him earnestly in my worst and limited Russian. I hoped that my expression would make up for my poor words of gratitude. He seemed to understand.

As I sat down and leaned against the inner wall, looking around at everyone and processing all that had happened, the GCTC lead came up to those of us remaining (those who hadn't succumbed to vomiting and were still capable of flying in Zero G) and shook our hands. It felt like we had all earned a little bit more respect from him. That we had passed this small rite of passage. It was a celebratory moment for us all and I was thrilled with myself that I had made it to the end. That I had enjoyed it so much more than I had expected. That I had completed all the work that I had planned to do, and still had time to play.

The plane landed and once the engines switched off we all excitedly shared our experiences, laughing together and helping each other disembark from the plane. Andreas ran up to us to hear how it all went. 'Did you get the shots?' he asked me. 'Did you get the footage that you needed?' 'Yes!' I told him. 'And so much more.' After a group photo, the GCTC team headed off and we were on our way back to the hotel.

As the adrenaline started to leave my body, I realised how completely knackered I was from the experience. Thankfully, time had been factored into our itinerary to rest post-flight, so after a light lunch, I went back to my bed and slept soundly for a few hours. I guess our bodies were working really hard against the 2G forces and then we were probably concentrating a lot when we were in Zero G. I found loads of bruises on my body, and it also felt like I had bruised some ribs, but I couldn't recall hurting myself throughout the flight. I got up for dinner and joined the table of my fellow Zero G passengers. There was lots of laughter and smiles and support. We had shared this special experience and it had brought us all together.

***

In addition to the Zero G experience, I also got to spend time at Star City, the training centre for astronauts in Russia. Visiting the GCTC the day after the flight, we saw the Soyuz and ISS training modules, the working centrifuges and medical training centres. All used by astronauts training for their missions to the International Space Station; whether from Roscosmos, ESA, NASA or CSA, they all trained at Star City.

The footage that I obtained from my Zero G flight was extraordinary and when I spliced together the segments of weightlessness during the flight it all came together really well. I was so proud of how I had coped during the flight. I had been terrified for most of it, but I'd refused to let it get to me. Again I had surprised myself with what I was capable of. Just like at MDRS, I found that I was hardier than I had previously realised. I was starting to really think that maybe I had the right stuff to get to space.

Andreas contacted me a few weeks after I returned home. He had watched the footage of the Zero G flight, seen the impact the trip had on me and also noted that people were engaging with me more online as a consequence of the posts I had shared about my experience on the Zero G flight. He asked me if I was serious about trying to get to space. He saw that I was tenacious and determined but also that, as an artist, I was approaching my mission to get to space from a different angle than others who shared a similar passion. He could see that I was indeed serious about devoting the rest of my life to fulfilling this enormous, near-impossible dream. He got it. He understood it. And he was keen to help me make it happen.

Getting that kind of feedback was a massive boost to me. It really shifted how I communicated my ambition; I started owning it more, started paring back any activities that weren't directly feeding into the quest. I needed to get more strategic when it came to time management. I began to see that if I could somehow gather together more people like Andreas, who knew the business of space well and believed in what I was trying to achieve, I might be able to pull this off.

***

Off the back of my work in communicating my Mars mission, the various talks and family events and broadcasting work that I had been a part of, my reputation among the space community as a communicator and artist began to grow.

My old pal Roy from MDRS invited me to be a part of the new analogue facility that he had built with his space science community who were already working together on the Young Astronaut Academy programme (these were the same students who had contacted us while we were on our mission at MDRS). As he had explained to us during our mission in 2017, he wanted to set up an analogue research station in his home country and use the facility to teach young adults about space. Learn by experience, if you will. There was heaps of support for this scheme and his architecture, engineering and scientific colleagues worked together to design, build and assemble their own Mars analogue in the Negev desert at the Ramon crater. They called it DMARS and Roy and his teammates wanted me to be a part of their first mission, in order to help them communicate effectively, documenting the astronauts' experience much like how we had done while at MDRS.

It was an opportunity that I couldn't decline and so in early February 2018 I headed off to the Negev desert. It was also a chance to see Roy again. I had missed him a lot since MDRS and was looking forward to spending time with him, visiting his kibbutz, Na'an, and meeting his family.

And more opportunities began to emerge for me to share my work with the general public. Science Gallery curated an exhibition in June 2018 focusing on living in the extremes, called 'Life on the Edge'. As well as acting as a consultant for part of their exhibition, I was also fortunate to create an installation for it. Inspired by my time at MDRS, I built a miniature habitat, re-creating within a limited space the living and working conditions of an analogue facility. Filled with personal items from our MDRS mission, recordings of our radio comms while on EVAs and other equipment used at analogue facilities, I tried to capture the essence of our existence while living together at MDRS.

But perhaps the most significant part of my continuing journey to get to space was my trip to Baikonur to witness a live launch from the Baikonur Cosmodrome.

Chapter 17

Getting to the Baikonur Cosmodrome

Frankfurt Airport Terminal 2 – Saturday 2 June 2018, 6.30 p.m.

This kid has completely captivated me. I think he is about fourteen or fifteen months old. He has a gorgeous moon face with big bright smiling eyes. He looks Kazak and is carelessly wobbling around the waiting area. His mother seems distracted; she's been consistently on the phone since we got here and seems to be travelling solo with him. He's wandering around the area where I'm sitting, looking around at everyone with this big friendly grin on him. I want him to see me smiling back at him. When he does, he beams back. He's a welcome distraction as I'm knackered. I've been hanging around Frankfurt Airport all day after having gotten an early flight from Dublin.

Eventually I leave the child and head back over to the group because I see that our fifth and final member has arrived. I really would prefer to have sat there, watching this fearless child, but I daren't. What would my travel companions think of me? I want to make a good first impression, after all.

I'm not sure if I've made the right decision in coming on

this trip. I've left myself financially vulnerable. It's not that I cannot afford it; I can. It's just that a ton of people are way overdue in payments to me. I think it's an omen.

Furthermore, I don't feel prepared for this trip; I haven't had the time to study Baikonur enough. I know Andreas, at least; we've been consistently Skyping since the Zero G flight last August. He seemed gruff when I met him first, but he's sound and I'm happy that he's here. He's never fully seen my playful, spontaneous side and I've decided to keep it under wraps for this trip as I want to reassure him that I'm a fully fledged responsible adult.

I've been in Stefan and Steffen's company for about thirty minutes now. They're German. Earlier, we were all hanging around the check-in counter, waiting for Andreas to arrive, and I could see that we all seemed to be waiting for the same person. So when Andreas turned the corner, sweaty and a little flustered, our group was immediately formed.

Steffen is a chemist. You can tell that he is fastidious in everything he does, and likely achieves anything that he sets his mind to. He's told me that he's a pilot too, that he wanted to apply to be an astronaut and wants to see the launch to make sure that ESA's Alexander Gerst does a good job. This guy is the real deal and I'm super-impressed.

Stefan and I have bonded over language and the way I confuse the meanings of German words. He's worried that his English isn't good enough, but I reassure him that I can keep up with a conversation in German (an admission I come to regret a couple of days later when a German TV company interviews us!). I haven't had time to ask him too much about why he's going to Baikonur, but I know that I'll have lots of time in the days ahead to get to know him.

Vasily is the last to join us. He seems flustered and I think that maybe he's had a stressful journey. I introduce myself and reassure myself that standing with them all is the right thing to do, rather than returning to my seat near the cute kid. I'm not really listening to the group's conversation, but I hear the odd word. Concrete comes up a lot; I think it's something to do with Vasily's job. So while I'm standing there, I can't help but turn back to watching the kid.

The cute kid has now approached another kid, grabbed them and kissed them squarely on the cheeks. I burst into laughter and the group stare at me. 'Sorry,' I say, 'there is this really cute kid. He's just grabbed another kid and kissed them. This little fella is amazing.' They smile meekly and there's a silence. 'You idiot!' I say to myself. 'Focus on the group, forget about the kid. You're making yourself look like an idiot.'

So I turn my attention to the group and listen intently to the concrete conversation, nodding where appropriate, as Andreas and Vasily wax lyrical about buildings or something. 'How did you get here?' I ask Vasily. 'I drove,' he replies. Then we go back to the concrete conversation.

Just then the cute kid approaches the group and stands beside us all, as if he's also fascinated by this concrete conversation. I crack up laughing again, and this time everyone else does as well. This little fella is super-cute. Then he laughs because we're all laughing. Then he grabs my leg and gives me an enormous hug and I absolutely melt. He's beaming up at me. I rub his lovely little head and his mum runs over and makes a gesture of apology. I want to tell her that it's fine, that I'm happy to have him beside me, but she takes him away.

**

We're boarding the flight to Astana. Andreas had wanted us all to sit together but that hasn't transpired. I'm going to be sitting on my own. In some ways, I feel bad that we're not together. But also I'm kind of relieved. In new groups, I put tons of energy into getting to know everyone, which is great, but for a long flight, I'm not sure if I can keep that up. It's probably easier for everyone that I'm sitting on my own.

A flight attendant takes the baby buggy off the cute kid's mother, to place in the hold of the plane during the flight. It leaves her with two overflowing plastic bags of blankets, bottles and other kid stuff that she needs to carry onto the plane. She scoops up the cute kid and is struggling to use her free hand to carry her bags. I offer to help, but she's happy to do it herself. As we're all shuffling slowly towards the gate now, I beckon her to move in front of us and I wave at the flight attendant that there's a mother and baby in need of priority boarding. She smiles and nods in thanks. I smile back, wave goodbye to the cute little kid, who has already moved on to the next distraction. I hope that we are sitting somewhere close together on the flight. But I never see them again.

I get to my seat. I'm sharing the row with just one other person. I think again about my new travel companions. They are nice people, already really easy to chat with. A bit serious for me, maybe. But I don't care. Because I'm finally going to see a real live rocket launch. With Alexander Gerst on the top of it as he heads to the International Space Station. Four years ago, I never would have imagined that I would be boarding a plane to Kazakhstan.

And for the first time in weeks, I feel like this is where I'm supposed to be. That this trip is going to be great.

Astana Airport – Sunday, 5.45 a.m.

I meet up with Steffen, Stefan, Andreas and Vasily in the concourse. It's weird. In the short time that we've been together, something has changed between us. We're a team now. Already. We're giddy, chatting away. No more 'concrete' chats happening, thankfully. Now we're noticing this new environment together, enjoying the sensory overload. 'Look at the Kazak police uniform!' Vasily says. 'Do you think I could get them to give me one of their oversized helmets?'

Our tiny visa forms get stamped at passport control by another uniformed policeman in a large helmet. We're told to keep them safe. And now we're officially in Kazakhstan! We're wandering around, drinking it all in – the buildings, the people, the shops. Vasily is already snapping away on his camera. Andreas shepherds us all towards the very small bureau de change. I exchange €150 for Russian rubles and €50 for Kazakh tenge. I hope it's enough.

We walk outside the airport to access Terminal 2. It's freezing outside, similar to a spring morning back home.

'Maybe the temperatures are going to be low after all. Not like the typical summer desert temperatures,' Steffen says. 'God I hope not,' I say. 'I didn't bring warm clothes with me.' I have brought light, summer clothes, as instructed by Andreas. Not even a heavy sweater. I wonder if I'll be able to buy clothes in Baikonur.

As we descend the stairs to the boarding gate for our next flight, it suddenly feels like we're back in Europe. Everyone here looks familiar, and I hear English and German being spoken, with the occasional big yelp of laughter bursting above the excited voices.

Our next step is to board a flight to Kyzylorda Airport. One step closer to our final destination of Baikonur. And it strikes me that all of us are here for the launch. There's a kinship between us all. A guy called Peter approaches me; he knows me from Twitter. I don't know him but appreciate that he's reached out to me.

'Everyone is here,' Andreas says.

People all seem to know each other; there are lots of handshakes and hugs. He disappears across the hall. Then I see Galina! The same guide that I had on the Zero G flight. I wave over at her, but she can't see me. She's surrounded by a big group of people. I imagine they are probably the Slovenians who are joining us on the trip. I'm looking forward to catching up with Galina.

Boarding Gate – 7 a.m.
The gate opens and people make a haphazard queue towards

the bus to take us to our flight. I feel part of this group already. Sort of. Maybe it's because we all share the same passion for space. There is no pushing and shoving; instead people are politely making room for everyone on the bus heading out to the final flight.

The bus to the plane is crammed: mostly men, maybe seven or eight other women. They're different from me; more outdoorsy types. A lot of them are wearing space-themed T-shirts or jackets. And warm sweaters, I notice, worrying again that I've brought the wrong clothes. One woman's voice is booming over the rest of us. I know by her demeanour that she's done this many times before: shouting across to different people, sharing jokes that make absolutely no sense to me. But everyone other than Stefan and me seem to find what she says hilarious.

The lady beside me looks totally out of place on this largely European bus. 'Excuse me,' she asks, 'do you mind if I ask you why you are here?' 'We're all here for a rocket launch in Baikonur,' I tell her. I notice people looking at me and hope that I pronounced Baikonur correctly. 'Ah,' she says, 'I understand now. I have never seen so many foreign people here before. Enjoy your time in Kazakhstan.' I say thank you and am about to ask her about her life here when the bus doors open and we are already at the plane. I never see her again.

Monday, 5.40 a.m.

When I wake I initially think that I'm at home in my own bed. I look around and remember where I am and that today we're going to see the Soyuz MS-09 rocket make its way across the cosmodrome to Launchpad #1, also known as Gagarin's Start. I bounce out of the bed, ready for this awesome day.

And soon we are off, heading to Baikonur Cosmodrome, where the Soyuz MS-09 will emerge from the factory at 7 a.m. We're running a little behind so the driver – a Kazak man who I never get to speak to, or even find out his name – drives like a maniac across the Steppe desert. We share the bus with a group of Slovenians, who are sitting down the back. They're bouncing even more than we are up front, and you can hear the occasional 'ow' when our driver goes over a bump in the road. The shock absorbers are well worn in this vehicle, so we're all feeling every move. Sometimes I think our driver is doing this on purpose. I suspect he gets a kick out of tossing us around like dice in his van.

The Sun is rising, making a gorgeous red haze on the horizon. It is cold this morning in the Steppe desert and so I wear as many layers as I can. Thankfully, my scarf and waterproof give me some warmth. Vasily is clicking away on his camera, as are many of the Slovenians, while the crazy Kazak drives maniacally to get us to Site #112 in time to witness the big reveal of the rocket that will launch in two days and take ESA's Alexander Gerst, NASA's Serena Auñón-Chancellor and Roscosmos' Sergey Prokopyev to the International Space Station.

The van eventually pulls up in a makeshift car park at the site. We all run to the railway line that emerges from the doors of a nearby factory. The energy has instantly shifted.

There are lots of excited voices and chats and laughter. There are about 150 people here, and they have all gathered at the main doors of the factory. We have already missed the unveiling of the rocket, as the doors are open, but thankfully it hasn't left the facility yet. We can already see the boosters, the big red cones at its base. It's a really beautiful sight. Some of the technical crew are walking around, casually ignoring us, setting the tone.

I brought my tripod and camera with me and am checking light settings when suddenly there's a huge hiss of steam, creaking of steel, and a thud of steel on steel. People around me start to click away. I look to my left and see that the rocket is on the move, slowly reversing out of the factory.

I feel like the rocket, in this moment, is an object of beauty, one we're all there to adore. The team of engineers and security personnel surrounding the rocket don't make eye contact with anyone, and just talk among themselves, almost like celebrities walking past on the red carpet. Some of them are wearing a navy uniform and weird headgear that looks like a motorcycle helmet, though they are wider and longer than a standard helmet.

I have a vague recollection that I've seen these people before. And then I realise that I've seen this ceremony before, this rolling out of the rocket, on TV. I remember these men in their strange navy helmets. It's old footage, grainy, but still in colour. I'm racking my brain trying to remember when I saw this before but can't. These navy-uniformed men and the other men in cream overalls know that we're all impressed by them, and their nonchalance is all part of the ceremony. As the rocket slowly passes us on a low trailer that is carrying it towards the launchpad, people are moving to keep pace with it, clicking away, not watching where they're going.

I'm not sure what I want to photograph, I can't get the whole view of this spectacle into one frame. And no picture I'm taking is doing justice to the sense of occasion. It feels like I'm on the shore, waving off the maiden voyage of the *Titanic* or something. I want to be a part of what's happening, but it's all so enormous that it's hard to grasp where I belong in it all.

We're told that the police and security staff don't like being photographed, and besides, they're enjoying corralling us too much. We're not allowed past a fence, even though the photographers with the telephoto lenses have already gone way beyond it. One of them barks at me, I don't know what was said, but I know I can't go any further. I look around and the place has cleared out. I don't see any of our team either.

The rocket is beautiful – for its engineering as much as the time and detail that has gone into its construction. It's hard to imagine that three people will be strapped into this in a few days' time. In fact, I really struggle to remember this the whole time I'm at Baikonur. The rocket is just so immense, and something that I have never seen in person before, that part of me can't process that its function is to transport people into space.

I head back to our van. Everyone is exhilarated by what we have just witnessed, checking each other's videos and pictures, smiling. Then we're off to the next stop along the way, to see the rocket head towards Gagarin's Start.

Railway Crossroads, 7.50 a.m.

Vasily is clicking away on his camera as we approach the railway crossing. We exit the van, seemingly well ahead of everyone else. We have staked out a good spot for ourselves, although honestly I can't decide where I want to go. In the far distance we can see Site #112 and the railway line that runs from the site in our direction. There's an Orthodox priest standing on the road. Andreas says that he's here to bless the rocket. I can't decide whether to stand where the priest is, or return to our main group.

The police are here again, with their bored faces. I have to say that I really like their uniform, which is like a navy set of army fatigues. I look at them, especially the trousers, and think that I'd love to own a pair. They'd be quite high fashion, especially if you wore them with heels. They have set up a barrier around the railway line that we cannot cross and they are walking up and down the other side of the barrier with their dogs, who look equally bored.

We stand here a long time, waiting to catch a glimpse of the rocket on the railway line. I'm standing with Vasily, while Steffen, Galina and Andreas are nearby. We are taking pictures of each other, of dogs, of the police, selfies, group photos, and we are chatting, getting to know each other better, so time ambles along quickly enough. And it's getting warmer too, meaning I can start to take off some of my layers.

Andreas tells us that we have the best spot and I soon realise that he's right. Busloads of people start to arrive, including one VIP bus filled with ESA, NASA, CSA and Roscosmos officials, former astronauts and friends and family of Alex, Serena and Sergey.

Someone taps me on the shoulder – it's Antonio Fortunato from ESA. We had met while I was at the Astronaut Centre the year before (I interviewed him as part of making *Diary of a Martian Beekeeper*). I also had arranged for him to come to Cork to give a lecture on mission control as part of SSP17. I had forgotten that he told me he would see me in Baikonur. He's always smiling, while also being very professional. Our relationship has always been work-related so I'm not sure how much I can ask him here – I want to meet all the astronauts who are with him just to view the launch and I want to ask him loads of questions about the crew and where they're going next. But I don't want to put him in an awkward position, so I let him lead the conversation. He tells me to keep an eye on the lower green part of the rocket and to tell him what I see on launch day. I tell him that I will. We get a picture together and then he returns to the VIP group.

By now, the rocket is quite close. The area is very busy and there are a lot more people here than there were at Site #112 – probably between 200 and 300, I'd say. We do indeed have a great view from where we are. There are two to three rows of people behind us. We're all clicking away again, trying to take that one perfect shot of the rocket. I'm changing between two lenses; one is a macro lens that's great for long-distance shots, but the clarity of that lens isn't as good as my other lens, which has a wide angle. I ultimately decide that my wide-angle lens is the better option.

With the rocket almost upon us, the back-up crew for the current mission gets out of the VIP bus and the police allow them to cross the barrier. Anne McClain of NASA, Oleg Kononenko of Roscosmos and David Saint-Jacques of CSA are just a little bit up from us, posing for pictures and being interviewed by TV reporters. David is particularly popular, it seems. If we were another five metres closer to the railroad crossing, I could get a picture with Anne McClain – I might even be able to chat to her – but it's not going to happen. We've made our choice of where to stand and if I move now, I'll lose the great viewpoint.

There's a whole reunion of astronauts happening behind me, especially with all the cosmonauts. Three German former astronauts are here too, and Stefan and Steffen are so excited to see them and be so close to them. Stefan manages to get a picture with one of them and is proudly sharing it with us all. It's a great moment for him and I wish that Sam Cristoforetti, or Paolo Nespoli or Tim Peake were here so I could have a moment like he has just experienced. Or Valentina Tereshkova even, the first woman in space, who launched from this very cosmodrome back in 1963. Valentina always takes me back to Yuri Gagarin and his huge achievement in being the first person ever in space. On 12 April 1961. I think about Yuri and Valentina, and the vast expanse of the cosmodrome and all that has been achieved here.

The rocket is finally upon us. As the Soyuz MS-09 passes by, Anne, Oleg and David salute it. We get another chance to view this wonderful piece of engineering before it arrives at the launchpad. Once it passes the railroad crossing, everyone jumps back in their vans and buses and we're off to the last part of the roll-out.

At Gagarin's Start, 10 a.m.

I'm beaming ear to ear now, very much feeling the spirit of the day, celebrating the arrival of this rocket to such an historic place. Launchpad #1 is where the very first artificial satellite was launched, the Sputnik, on 4 October 1957. It's also where Yuri launched into space for the very first time on the Vostok 1. And also where Valentina launched from too, two years later, aboard the Vostok 6. So many shape-shifting moments in space exploration. All from this site. And now I'm here, standing on this very launchpad, watching Alex's rocket being hoisted into place for his mission launch. It's a fabulous feeling and again I don't know what I want to film or photograph. It feels like I can't possibly capture it properly. But, like everyone else, I try.

Launchpad #1 is packed with the same people from earlier. I even recognise some of them from the airport. And just like at the railway crossing, astronauts and dignitaries are interspersed among us, all here to witness the Soyuz being hoisted into position, where it will remain until Alex, Serena and Sergey arrive in two days' time.

It takes almost seven minutes for the Soyuz MS-09 to be erected. I film it, realising halfway through that it's just that little bit too long for anyone to want to bother watching it again. But I continue filming it anyway, because that's what everyone else is doing.

I'm separated from my group again and am eavesdropping on loads of conversations around me. Someone very senior from NASA is behind me; he's with friends, it seems. They're taking pictures together, but I hear him ask his companions a few times not to post them publicly and they reassure him that they won't. I want to turn around to see who it is, but then he will know that I've been eavesdropping, so I keep my head forward.

I eventually head back to the group and we are brought behind the launchpad to a special monument to the Sputnik. There's a little boy there in a NASA spacesuit. He's precocious. I'm not sure whether he loves space or whether his parents thought that it would just be cute and eye-catching to put him in the suit. He's about six. I see him again at launch day. We never connect. And neither of us care.

***

It's almost too much to take in, the morning. I get swept up in the ceremony of it, and it is difficult to process what I am witnessing. That this rocket will soon have three people in it.

That this rocket is a mode of transport. That the design and engineering of the Soyuz has emerged from a rich legacy of over fifty years of Russia's best engineers and scientists. And that I'm going to see it launch in a matter of days. My brain is simply incapable of taking all that in, so I'm coasting along on the spectacle of it all. I'll think about it more later, I reassure myself, at a quieter time. If one comes.

Chapter 18

The Live Launch

Baikonur Cosmodrome, 6 June 2018
Outside Building 154: Two Hours to Launch

Our Roscosmos guide waves his pass and we are allowed through to a cordoned-off area outside the building, where only friends and family and space officials have access. I have a wonderful view of where the astronauts will emerge from the building on their way to the official bus that will drive them to the rocket. I am right in the front row, behind the official rope. We appear to have a whole section to ourselves.

It's a very warm day. Security are managing the crowd very well, all of us kept in our place. We wait a long time, standing in the hot sun, but I'm not prepared to give up my good spot. It's worth it when, after about an hour, Alex, Serena and Sergey emerge from the building in their Sokol suits. It's an image I've seen many times online, but now it's happening in front of me, mere metres away.

It doesn't seem real, somehow. Directly across from me stand Alex's family. As Alex walks past, I realise that this is their last moment together prior to the launch. And I think about how hard that must be, for both family and crew. I look at Alex's parents – they are smiling thinly, their fear somewhat disguised, though the eyes reveal the truth.

Suddenly my clear view is obscured by the press and some other people. I'm expecting security to order them back behind the rope, but it's not happening. As soon as the crew approach the nearby bus to take them to the rocket, everyone pushes forward even more and by the time the bus doors close I'm one of the few people left standing in my original place. I give in and rush forward to wave them off. I catch Alex staring down at his family, his hands in white gloves touching the glass. I watch Alex as he keeps his eyes fixed on them. Even among all these people it is an intimate moment and a part of me is ashamed that I don't look away.

The bus pulls out, headed to Launchpad #1. People run behind it until it turns a corner and is gone. Alex's family are left, still standing together and hugging each other as everyone else scarpers away. I want to go over to them, to wish them well, but who am I to them?

I hear Andreas call, 'Niamh, come! We have to go! Come! Come now!'

I look back – only the families and a few officials are left in this open space. I run to catch up with the group. And we are rushing across the Steppe again, in our van with magnificently bad suspension, headed towards our viewing area.

T Minus 10 to Launch

We have moved to the viewing area, just 800 metres from the launchpad. There are about 150 people in total standing with us in the middle of the desert steppe; we've all been afforded a top spot from which to view the launch. All thanks to Andreas. There's a screen with a countdown clock about twenty metres in front of us. The screen occasionally streams the live feed from the Soyuz, allowing us to see Alex, Serena and Sergey in the modules, waiting patiently for their moment to launch.

People are chatting away, always keeping one eye on the rocket. The rocket still looks immense from here. A rocket that now contains three souls. I suddenly remember what Antonio told me to do two days previously at the roll-out of the rocket. I look for the green lower section of the rocket, but see that it is now white, the result of a condensed moisture that gathers on the exterior of the fuel-filled rockets. My camera is all set up on the tripod; everything is ready to go. I also have my phone fully charged to take pictures. Andreas is also taking footage for all of us and has a GoPro mounted to the top of his camera. The amount of camera equipment in this field is extraordinary. There's a real buzz now, with just minutes to go.

'Remember this moment,' Andreas says quietly. 'You will never forget your first launch at Baikonur. It's a very special thing, especially for you.'

I nod, not quite sure what he means.

T Minus 1 to Launch

This is it. This is the moment that we've all been waiting for. The whole trip has been building up to this. I check my camera one last time and press record.

T Minus 10 Seconds

A male Russian-sounding voice comes over the tannoy. It's the ten-second countdown. The initial spark. The rumble. A huge explosion that overflows to the right of the rocket. Vibrations, a wobble in the rocket, then a move upwards, slowly first, and then boom, it's off. Into the sky! Going faster, faster, faster. The brightness of the rockets burning, the power, the heat and light on my face, the ground rumbling – to witness such speed, to know that three people are at the top, three people who are tiny in comparison to this huge rocket, it overwhelms me.

The moment of launch explodes into my brain. I glance to my camera, I've forgotten to move it to follow the rocket, the focus is off. I try to keep taking pictures as well, but it's too much to do. Sod it. I give up the camera and just watch the rocket sprint up into the air. It's all happening too fast. I want remember all of this. But it's not possible.

The sound of the rocket is exquisite: this dripping, popping constant drum. No one is speaking. I quickly glance around and see that everyone is watching the rocket behind a device of some sort. I have an overwhelming urge to scream and whoop and dance and cheer. But I know that I'd ruin everyone else's experience if I did. 'Go! Go! Go!' I whisper instead. 'Go!' I say, as I raise my hands in the air and throw my shoulders back.

The first stage of the Soyuz – the iconic four boosters – separates and onwards the rocket goes. It seems so small now. I'm trying to imagine them in there, what they are feeling and experiencing. I feel an overwhelming sense of pride. The achievement of it all. I'm so proud to be a human, to celebrate this moment.

Those first three minutes, as I watch them climb up, up and away, are magnificent. From then on we peek at the live stream from inside the Soyuz and then look back at the sky. As the Russian voice tells us that the second stage has separated, it is still so very quiet around me. No one dare celebrate without the all clear.

Then the Russian voice comes back on the tannoy and we're told that the launch has been a success. The third stage has stopped firing. Video of the crew comes through: weight-lessness has kicked in and they seem relaxed. Eight-and-a-half short but very long minutes have passed, and Alex, Serena and Sergey are on their way to the International Space Station.

Around me, people are cheering, hugging, comparing footage and chatting feverishly about how it all went. 'A perfect launch', 'flawless', 'couldn't have gone better', I hear. Andreas shouts, 'Group photo! Everyone, come here, we need to take a group photo.'

I don't want to be in a group photo; I'm not ready yet. I want everything to be quiet again, the way it was just a few moments ago. I want to see it again. I start to walk away, towards the launchpad and away from the crowd. Because I'm crying and I don't want anyone to see me. I have so many thoughts spinning in my head; I need some time to absorb them all. Vasily catches up with me and motions for me to come back for the photo. Galina is also nearby; she sees that I'm crying and hugs me. 'What? You're crying?' barks Andreas. 'In all my years of launches I've never seen that reaction before.' But he knows me and I think he understands as he edges away to leave me on my own. I want to hold on to the experience for a little longer.

I grab my phone, press record and make a small video.

The launch has completely overwhelmed me. I am excited and sad and hopeful and desperate and jealous and frustrated all in the same moment. Watching those three astronauts launch a mere 800 metres away has made my goal feel all the more real. And tantalisingly close. But I also realise that today I was on the wrong side of the fence. I now better appreciate the enormity of the task that's ahead of me, and, as I gather myself together and walk back to the group, I am more determined than ever to keep going.

In the van back to the hotel we toast the mission with vodka – a Russian tradition, seemingly. A little bit squiffy from the alcohol, I stick my head out the only window in this desperately stuffy van. It is one of those moments of total and utter contentment, that lovely calm of happiness and joy.

Once back at our hotel in Baikonur, I see that the lobby is full of ESA personnel, already celebrating the launch. Romain is there, whom I know from the Astronaut Centre, and Jules Grandsire, communications officer from the centre, and more. And Antonio too. There are hugs all around and smiles and sighs of relief now that everything has gone well. I'm invited to the ESA party, but I prefer to spend my last evening with my own Baikonur crew. Later on, at our favourite restaurant, we vow to return to Kazakhstan for Alex's landing. We think that it might be in October. That's a busy month for me, with Space Week and preparations for Science Week. But I don't care, I'll figure out a way of returning.

Epilogue

Overall, 2018 was a good year. I made headway in gaining recognition for my work – getting invitations to speak at larger events, including New Scientist Live and WIRED Next Generation in the UK, as well as from NASA Johnson at their Cross Industry Innovation Summit. People seemed interested in my unique story. I even received an invitation to appear on RTE's *The Late Late Show* to share my progress so far, as well as the unique way in which I was approaching my dream.

It's moments like this that really help shine a light on my quest and also indicate how far I have already come. For my parents and supporters, these moments are encouraging; they allow them to see that I am making headway, which means they may worry a little bit less about what I am doing with my life, and see that maybe it isn't a pointless quest. They are great moments to celebrate together.

I'm also aware of how much further I have yet to go in order to fulfil this huge goal. The support and exposure is so important, but I've realised – particularly in the last year – that it's just as important to share the challenges and difficult times as well as the successes. Setbacks, like my return to Kazakhstan, have become a vital part of the project too.

***

The week before Christmas 2018, I headed back to Kazakhstan to witness Alexander Gerst return to Earth having completed his six-month mission aboard the International Space Station. Joining him would be his crewmates, NASA's Serena Auñón-Chancellor and Roscosmos' Sergey Prokopyev, returning in the Soyuz MS-09 descent module, the same craft that I had witnessed launch on 6 June in Baikonur.

On 19 December, a group of us headed to Karaganda, the planned landing zone for the spacecraft, which was expected the following morning at 11.03 a.m. We were warned to bring our warmest clothes, as temperatures could drop to as low as minus fifty degrees Celsius at night. It was another expensive trip, and as ever, I worried that I may have over-extended myself. Everything that I had earned since the summer had gone towards it, and I still needed to borrow money from a friend to cover it all. But I felt that it would be worth it, to have witnessed a human mission to space at the moment of launch and the moment of return. While Christmas spirit was all around, this trip was the only thing that I was tuned into.

It was lovely to see Andreas and Stefan, my Baikonur pals from the summer, and Markus, whom I had met on the Zero G trip, again. Andreas told us that his colleagues thought that we were crazy to attempt to go to the steppe in the winter. I didn't care. I couldn't wait to get back there. We were going to be able to see the descent module for ourselves, touch it, see that charred exterior, the flimsy frame that protected the astronauts from the bubble of 1600-degree-Celsius plasma that surrounds the spacecraft on re-entry.

The plan was that we would get up early on Thursday morning and meet up with the vehicles heading into the steppe to assist in collecting the crew when they landed. From Karaganda, where we were stationed, that was approximately a forty-kilometre trip. And we would be ready to go at a moment's notice.

But on the evening before the planned re-entry, a heavy blizzard fell in Karaganda. And to avoid the threat of this weather affecting the landing, Roscosmos had no choice but to make a last-minute decision to change the landing zone to a site 400 kilometres further west. We were trapped in the Karaganda blizzard with a bracing temperature of minus thirty-six degrees Celsius. After several hours attempting to figure out alternative arrangements to get us closer to the new landing zone, we finally gave up at 2 a.m., accepting that we weren't going to make it. I wasn't going to see that spacecraft for myself after all.

I didn't sleep a wink that night. I was so disappointed that I had travelled so far and spent so much money to see this re-entry. How was I going to make this work? Simply put, I couldn't. I had to accept the circumstances and make the most of it.

We quietly watched Alex's return to Earth together

that morning on our phones in the restaurant of our hotel, delighted to see that they returned safely. Nothing about space is straightforward, after all.

There it was again, coming to mind – my own form of 'Normalisation of Deviance', the assumption that since everything had gone so well in the past, I could therefore get comfortable regarding the threat of failure in the future. I realised how terribly naive I'd been, and that dealing with failure was something I still needed to work on. I was reminded of the TEDx talk that I had given in UCD way back in 2014 and how failure had to be part of the process. That there is no real failure as long as I'm walking forward. Remembering that helped a lot. It was still a tough lesson, of course, but this realisation was probably the most valuable aspect of my return trip to Kazakhstan. (I'm still paying back that loan my friend gave me too. Hard lessons indeed.)

**

Space is incredibly dangerous, more than a lot of us know. Leaving this planet and staying alive is the single biggest achievement of any expedition to space. In June 2018, in the desert steppe, as I witnessed that launch of astronauts Gerst, Auñón-Chancellor and Prokopyev, I saw just how vulnerable humans are in those rockets. How much they entrust to the talented engineers and scientists who have planned their missions in minute detail, to eliminate, as much as humanly possible, any room for error. Because, in space, errors have potentially fatal consequences.

Here's how Commander Chris Hadfield described a launch at a BT Young Scientist event in 2014:

During lift-off the acceleration is so great that you clear the sixty-metre launch tower (more than twice the length of the Spire on O'Connell St in Dublin) in seconds, already travelling at 160 km per hour, unable to move any part of your body because of the G-force. Some are known to vomit such is the force on your body. Up and up you go, faster and faster! And after about six minutes you feel as if you weigh six times heavier, as acceleration pushes you, pins you in to your seat, climbing towards 40,000 km/hr or 11km/sec to break through Earth's gravitational pull. And then eight-and-a-half minutes, as you leave Earth's atmosphere, the engines turn off and you instantly go from feeling really heavy to suddenly feeling weightless. And you have survived launch.

I experienced ten episodes of forty-second spurts of weightlessness on a parabolic flight in Star City, Moscow in 2017. I found it, even in that limited experience, to be exhausting, confusing, nauseating, exhilarating, terrifying and magnificent all at once. It gave me a much better appreciation of how difficult it must be for astronauts to work, sleep, eat or undertake any normal daily activities while in space. To adapt to a daily life of weightlessness is no mean feat and this is the least of our troubles if we are to consider the logistics of exploring space.

Take spacewalks (or EVAs): if your spacesuit begins to

fail and you are directly exposed to space, it is estimated that you have – at best – about ten minutes to live. But even within ten seconds the reduced pressure would begin to boil your blood. At the Mars Desert Research Station, while on EVAs, the logistics of suiting up were difficult and time-consuming. And then attempting to collect samples in our suits or even manoeuvre around the landscape was awkward and exhausting. I completed EVAs on Earth, where the actual danger of EVAs conducted in the vacuum of space under different gravity conditions was not something I needed to consider. The dangers for humans in space, anywhere off-Earth, cannot be underestimated. And yet, despite that – in fact, because of that – I want to play a part in our history of human space exploration.

After all, space has been my greatest love in life. Since 2011, after a thirty-year hiatus, I've been on this quest, and without any doubt, it's been the most challenging chapter of my life but also definitely the most rewarding, joyful and enriching. It's been a long, slow process of making small adjustments to my perception of my place in the world and in space, and, most of all, to the value that I put on myself. A process instigated by that day back in 2011 when I put on that flight suit, but activated by the desire to confront myself once and for all.

I have never worked so hard, been so vulnerable and tired, and felt so pushed to my limit, while also feeling so deter-mined, happy, open-hearted, generous, creative, inquisitive, collaborative and unafraid. And proud. I'm finally proud of who I am and what I stand for. I believe in what I'm doing and my commitment to and belief in it have only deepened over the years. I get braver with every new piece that I make, every talk I give or workshop I share. Every new adventure, every new challenge. So let me explain, as best as I can, what it is exactly that I want to ultimately achieve in getting to space.

I often think about that *Earthrise* picture taken in 1968 of our planet Earth and how it was a moment that revealed a new perspective for people, a new way of seeing. The picture stimulated a seismic moment for many, one believed to have kick-started the whole environmental movement. By seeing Earth from this different vantage point, people suddenly saw Earth differently. Every astronaut that I have researched or met has spoken about the impact this new vantage point had on their view of Earth. Frank White called it the 'Overview Effect'. I like to think that it's a moment of clarity.

My mission is about providing another moment of clarity by allowing everyone to see the journey to get to space from a fresh perspective. Astronauts respect their role as custodians of the work and efforts of others, so they don't grumble or complain, they do not expose how truly frail we are as humans when taken out of our comfort zone, how vulnerable we are in space. But what would it be like to see someone really struggling? What would it be like to see someone 'normal' in space?

I'm someone who, I believe, has the skills to share this journey from start to end, with honesty, vulnerability, fear, hesitancy and excitement. I'm someone who hasn't been trained to work in space but knows enough engineering and science to survive there (just about) and who can explain the experience in a familiar way. I believe that I'm someone whose story can appeal not only to those who already have a passion for science and space, but also to the general public who think that space and science isn't for them. What if they saw a person who they connected with, someone who felt more familiar to them, attempting to go to space? What would that do? How would it change our perception of ourselves on Earth? And our relationship with space? It's possible that it could remind us that together we can make the impossible possible; we can challenge the norm, and find a new way of seeing ourselves.

A vital part of this quest, for me, is that I earn the right to do this. I can't make this happen without people believing in what I'm trying to do; the opportunity has to emerge from my work on Earth. This mission of mine – to follow my dream, to get to space – is an art experiment of sorts, or a 'life experiment'. It's never been about simply getting to space. It isn't about being the 'first' to have this single experience and then return to Earth as a new astronaut. It is my life's work: to see what would happen if I finally stopped being afraid and pursued my biggest dream. It's about seeing what happens when I just try. It's about the odds being stacked against me, about not being the likeliest candidate, being too old, not fit enough, not skilled enough, not wealthy enough, being the outsider. It's about making an advantage out of these disadvantages. It's about creating something that the world at large feels a part of, because they know me from following my efforts, my years of work in communicating space, sharing my story with as many people as possible. This is about sharing the bad days, the frustrations, the disappointments and the failures. Sharing all of it. Giving people everything so that somehow they will see me, see what I'm trying to achieve, and want to be a part of it.

And so the point of the experiment is to just keep moving forward. I'm aware that the budget for my mission – however I manage to get it – will be difficult to raise without some sort of philanthropic financial intervention. But it's vital to me to earn the right to go to space – and to do so I must be part of a project that has value and merit for society at large. I believe my experiment potentially has such a value.

As of yet, there has been no mission to send an artist to space, which is essentially what I'm trying to do. A mission to the Moon as artist and communicator, or, more feasibly, a short mission to the International Space Station. A mission where my role would be to share every moment of the experience with my followers and supporters, preparing the mission together, seeing Earth from a distance together. And then seeing what could possibly emerge from that shared experience after the mission ends. That's it, that's the quest.

Many space agencies already appreciate and value the contribution of artists who focus on space in their work. I'm sure that if the agencies had the budget, and the instruction was given by their governing bodies to proceed, artists would be visiting space. We do have art pieces on the Moon and many art projects have been launched into space in recent years. It was encouraging to see Yusaku Maezawa announce in 2018 his 'Dear Moon' project – to invite eight artists with him on SpaceX's first mission to orbit the Moon, scheduled for 2024. It's difficult to know exactly when or even if this will take place, but if it does, I truly believe that a lot could come from this mission. And who knows, maybe I'll be a part of it – or another mission just like it. All the more reason to keep trying, keep pushing, keep working hard.

***

Everything worth doing always comes at a cost. I question myself daily about what I'm doing, about the sacrifices I've made. I've gotten used to feeling afraid all the time; it comes with the territory of taking risks. The lack of money is a real fear too, the worry that one day I'll have to stop because I can't make it work any more. But I need to see this through to the end, whatever that end is. Maybe, one day, I'll achieve it and I'll get to space. Or maybe I'll be on my deathbed and will still be trying to make it happen. Who knows? But until that day arrives, I will continue to give everything to this quest, because that's the point of this 'life experiment'. And I want that work to be my legacy, the evidence of my existence, that I made a mark on the world, that I made a difference. It has come at a massive cost, but I know after many years of deliberation that it is my most truthful and rewarding existence.

Maybe all of this emanates from that little eight-year-old who believed in herself more than I did as an adult. Maybe it's partly about seeking acceptance from those girls at Scoil Eoin

Baiste who squeezed oranges on my face, pushed me, jeered me, thought that I was nothing. Maybe it's about proving to myself that my choices to step away from academia, from countless relationships and from acting, and all the other big life decisions that I made, were worth it. That I was right to be lost for all those years. To be honest, I'm not sure whether it really matters any more. What does matter is that, for whatever reason, this desire to get to space – once acknowledged – is the fuel that has driven me to never give up, even when I was terrified of pursuing the dream.

I think that we can be many things. It is okay to change our minds, to make mistakes. There are so many different ways to live our lives and so many paths from which to choose. It is important to realise that confronting our fears can set us free. That our reality is often based on our perceptions and that we can change those perceptions at any time. That the true reward in life is the effort in working hard towards something that truly matters to us.

So, like I asked you at the start of this book – where are you right now? I imagine you are probably in a room in your house, or in your place of work, or on a train or bus, or a plane, or even a boat. Maybe you're outside in your garden, or in a park in the city. We're in different places but, wherever we are, we are both occupying a tiny piece of space on the same planet. And to know that, to realise how truly tiny we are in this universe, gives me a tremendous sense of freedom. I think that we're all part of something much bigger than ourselves. In the story of our universe, we exist for such a very short period of time, so it's up to us to create the very best life for ourselves and to each leave our own legacy for the next generation to build upon.

I had a moment of clarity in 2011 that changed the course of my life. What I've learned from all of this is that we can choose to do something in those moments, or not. The important thing is to acknowledge those moments and to make peace with your choice. Let them go, or pursue them. But don't ignore them. They'll haunt you if you do. And there are always costs involved. So don't wait around. Don't waste precious years thinking about the 'what ifs'. Waiting is failing. Success is walking forward. Live a life that has meaning to you. And embrace it all – the good and the bad.

I've never felt more alive, or terrified, or vulnerable, or brave. Each day I learn more and more about how I can best contribute to the world and leave my mark. And it brings me such joy. I heard the very wise Commander Chris Hadfield once say, 'Life is at best a lottery. So the real question is, do you allow yourself the audacity of a dream?'

Space has been the love of my life and I believe that I'll get there one day. I don't know how. Or when. But when I do, you'll be with me. In all of it, every nitty gritty detail from start to finish. For it will all be for nothing if that journey is not shared.

In the 1990s, five space agencies came together
to create a living laboratory in space that orbits 330km
above us.
The same distance between Dublin and Manchester.
Their objective? To gain a better understanding of space
and of what we need to know to increase our chances of
survival off Earth.

That place is called the International Space Station
and has been running since 2000.
Equipped with science laboratories, a telescope, supplies
and support systems for its six-to-eight manned crew,
it's the first HOME we have created for ourselves outside
Earth's atmosphere.
An orbiting outpost.

The crew spends their free time
in the Cupola.
Sneaking a peek whenever they can
down to Earth.

The Cupola.
My favourite thing ever.
It's a window on the ISS,
with the best possible views of our planet.

When I'm on the ISS that's where I'd go on my break.
To the Cupola.
To eat my peanut butter pitta pocket.
Cos that's what they eat on the ISS.
Maybe one of my crew might join me.
Vlad from Roscosmos.

A cosmonaut. That's what Russians call their astronauts:

How'ya Vlad?
Doesn't get any better than this does it?
Best. Gig. Ever.

What's that?
Oh, did I not already tell you how I got here?
Oh, I'm sorry.

Well it's an interesting story.
Basically I made this show
about space
called To Space
which premiered at the Tiger Fringe Festival in Dublin
in 2014.
And it was a huge success; the response was incredible –
rave reviews, standing ovations.
Anyway next thing I know we're on a massive world tour
playing at all the big venues – Sydney Opera House,
Carnegie Hall, Albert Hall.

And after our second tour of eighteen months straight,
I came home.
And I was sitting there having a cup of tea
when the phone rang.
It was Jan Wörner.
Yes, that's right – the director general of ESA!

And he said:
'Guten tag, Niamh, wie gehts? Vielen dank für was haben
sie mit spazionen gemacht –'
Oh, sorry, Vlad, I forgot that you don't speak German.

He said:
'Niamh, congratulations!
What an achievement!
Thank you – for communicating space to a whole new audience.
We at ESA really feel that we need to reward you for what you've done.
So I have something I'd like to run by you.
Now I know how busy you are, but just think about this for a bit.'

'We are in the process of establishing an artist in residence for ESA
and we were considering two artists for this position.
I mean, they're not as great as you, you might know them: Marina Abramović and Philip Glass?
Anyway, we were having our final meeting and deciding who we should award it to
when Lorraine [Conroy] burst in and said
"Stop! What about Niamh?"
And we knew immediately that she was right.
Because it IS you, Niamh.
It's ALWAYS been you.
So what do you say?
Would you be our artist in residence?'

And here I am.
I get to come up here whenever I want.

What's that?
What would I have done if that hadn't happened?

Wow!
Well, it's interesting
because in 2014 I looked on the ESA website
and checked out the criteria for astronaut selection.
And I initially thought that I met all the criteria:
a degree in engineering,
a PhD in science.
But over that year, as I pursued it further,
it turned out that I needed a first-class honours
from a reputable college like MIT or somewhere like that.

And my PhD wasn't really suitable either – they really
wanted one in astrophysics, or astrobiology, not food
science.
And that they're ideally looking for people in their
twenties when they apply.
So if I had applied that way, I wouldn't have made it
here.

And if it wasn't for this ISS residency?
I guess I would have carried on.

I still would have made a show in 2014 about space.
I'd still be looking for ways to get to space.

But sure I'm here now anyways.

– Closing scene from *To Space*, 2014

Acknowledgements

This is a nice opportunity to thank those who have helped, supported and championed me since I started out on my big space quest.

I need to thank my friends and family, for who are we without the people we love? I'm standing where I am today because of all of you. So here we go. Mam and Dad, thanks for encouraging me to be curious, to devour life with passion and, most of all, to be a good person at all costs. To John, Tom, Deirdre, John K, Ciara, Stephen, Lorna, Sarah, Patricia, Padraic, Anna, Donal, Alison, Alison and Christian for our shared passion for curiosity, technology and sci-fi and for your never-ending support and love. To my dear friend Michael, who has been there for me more years than I care to admit and makes me laugh harder than any person I've ever known. To my dearest pal and pseudo-sister Orlaith and her gorgeous family for having my back, sharing her wise insights and being there always. To Olive for really getting it, to Karen at Unit K for that keen eye and shared passion for space, and to Colm for your limitless support.

To my crew at CIT Blackrock Castle Observatory, especially my friend and colleague Clair McSweeney, and Niall Smith, who welcomed me into their beautiful castle of space in 2013 and gave me a home as their artist in residence for five years, thereby allowing me to begin my journey in earnest. To Vince and Ellen from the Festival of Curiosity for their friendship and unending support as my wise and insightful mentors and advisers – thank you also for daring to change the world. To Stephanie O'Neill, Cathy Foley, Margie McCarthy and Ruth Freeman at Science Foundation Ireland for their support of my work in theatre and STEAM activities. To Kevin Nolan, Ger McNaughton and Katie Molony – the chats we had were invaluable to me and thank you so much for your wisdom, encouragement and focus. To Josh Richards, a kindred spirit and fellow ginger who tirelessly championed me back in the early days and introduced me to the space community at large.

Special thanks to my supporters at the European Space Agency, especially the amazing Lorraine Conroy, Karen O'Flaherty, Ruth McAvinia, Matt Taylor and Mark McCaughrean at ESA ESTEC. Thanks also to Juan de Dalmau, now at the International Space University, and to Aidan Cowley, Romain Charles, Jules Grandsire and the staff at ESA's Astronaut Centre. To astronauts Paolo Nespoli (ESA), Bob Thirsk (CSA) and Alexander Gerst (ESA) for providing interviews and access to their work and life on board the ISS. To Ian Harkin and Isla McMcGuckin at the Lottie Doll Company. To my Space Studies Program pals: John Connolly, Omar Hatamleh, Chris Welch, Geoff Steeves, Goktug. To Andreas at Space Affairs (and his team on the ground), who has even bigger dreams than I do and who constantly encourages me, inspires me and motivates me to keep going, to be realistic and to never give up. To my SSP Irish alumni, and my new international space pals, especially Elburz, Oriol and Saho, who showed me a new way of working, exploring and adapting, and who educated me in new technology, as well as showing me how to think bigger and how hard work can make anything possible.

And, of course, my amazing Crew 173: Arnau, Michaela, Idriss, Rick and Roy. They are my special family of friends who experienced with me those fifteen incredible Sols on Mars in the Utah desert in 2017. The mission continues to inspire me. Thanks again for taking such great care of me when I was completely out of my comfort zone, for all the great meals and stories, but mostly for all the laughter during those long days and nights at MDRS. Our MDRS experience would not have been possible without the following people who supported us all the way: Shannon Rupert, Robert Zubrin, the full CAPCOM crew during our mission; thanks also to all involved in the Mars Desert Research Station facility, Utah. We also acknowledge the support of our sponsors: The Israeli Space Agency (Israel), SOSA (Slovakia), O'Sol (France), the Weizmann Institute of Science (Israel), Purdue University (USA), the University of New South Wales (Australia), the International Space University (France), Slovenské Elektrárne (Slovakia), Ministerstvo školstva, vedy, výskumu a športu Slovenskej Republiky (Slovakia), Kozí Vŕšok (Slovakia), Team-Active (France), the Australian Centre for Astrobiology (Australia) and Teach on Mars (France). Plus, I'd like to thank those who privately supported the mission, including:

Hugh Byrne (Ireland), Marie Hélene Bernier (Canada), Reinhard Tlustos (Austria), Lars Hoving (Netherlands), François Ferre (France), Pankaj Pagare, Annette Winkler and Perrin Rynning. We are eternally grateful.

To my family of artists and theatre makers who have helped me create *Diary of a Martian Beekeeper* (2017), *To Space* (2014) and *That's About the Size of It* (2011). Without your support and input this work would not exist, so my sincere thanks to Sarah Baxter, Aoife White, Joanna Crawley, Ronan Phelan, Dan Colley, Liadain Ni Chearbhaill, Conor Burnell, Ger Clancy, Aine O'Hara, Mick Cullinan, Bill Woodland, Hugo Simoes, as well as Una Kavanagh, Louise Lowe and Owen Boss at ANU Productions. Thanks also to Ciaran Walsh and all at Culture Ireland and the theatre department of The Arts Council of Ireland for their support in making and touring this work nationally and internationally. Thanks also to the following organisations for the opportunities afforded me in creating this work: Arts@CERN, Science Gallery Dublin, Show in a Bag, MAKE, Theatre Forum, Irish Theatre Institute, Fishamble: The New Play Company, Dublin Fringe Festival and Dublin City Council Arts Office.

To my oldest and dearest Craic Pack comedy improvisers: Peter, Dermot, Rachel, Sharon, Danny, Keith, Graeme, Aidan and John, and my Snatch Comedy Cork crew: Marcus, Adrian, George, Damian and Cathal. Special mention to some of my The Second City LA improv teachers and colleagues: Dave Razowsky, Kevin Guzowski and Alan Hawkins. You all showed me in my thirteen years of improv how to be brave in my decisions, to embrace failure and say 'Yes, and' to every offer. But mostly you showed me how to be a better human being.

Further thanks must go to the wide network of science communicators: the late great Mary Mulvihill, Brian Trench, Ann O'Dea (InspireFest), Caroline Gill and Micheal Whelan (TEDxUCD), Shaun O'Boyle, Claire O'Connell, Alex Boyd (UCD), Simon Elliott and Fergus McAuliffe (UCD), and Liz McBain from the British Council in Ireland.

To my supporters at NASA. Thanks especially to Gary Martin, John Connolly, Omar Hatamleh and Michael Interbartolo. Thanks to the teams of people at Roscosmos, the Gagarin Research & Test Cosmonaut Training Center in Star City, Moscow and at the Baikonur Cosmodrome, especially Alla and Galina.

To Frances and Joanne at Personally Speaking for rooting for me always. To Lorraine, Louise and all at Lorraine Brennan for all the voiceovers and acting jobs over the years.

To my teachers, lecturers and mentors over the years, especially Sr Louis Marie and Mrs Greer. Thanks for encouraging me to keep questioning, keep exploring.

Thanks to little Hayden and his mother, Caroline Geraghty, for all the lovely paintings and messages of support since meeting them in 2017.

Since I began writing this book, three colleagues of mine left this world far too soon: to Dave Fahy, Julie McCann and Karl Shiels – you left a big impact on many of us and we'll never forget you.

A huge thanks to RTÉ Radio and TV for all the science

slots across your programme schedule over the years, and to *The Ryan Tubridy Show* and the teams at *The Late Late Show* and *The Tommy Tiernan Show* for providing me with such a public platform to share my space quest with Ireland.

To Peter, for his thirteen years of devotion and selfless love, for putting me back together, for supporting me along my journey, for being there with me every step of the way, holding my hand until I was ready to walk forward on my own. A special thanks to you for being my very best friend, and for knowing when it was time to set me free. I would not be here without those many years of encouragement and reinforcement.

Lastly, to Mercier Press for believing that I have a story to tell and for coaxing me gently and patiently along the process. I'm forever grateful to Pa O'Donoghue for inviting me to have a coffee in 2018 and for giving me the encouragement to just try to put some words down on a page. Thanks also to the talent and insight of editor Noel O'Regan – together we somehow managed to create a book about this very long and winding tale of space.

Thanks everyone!